PRACTICE – ASSESS – DIAGN[OSE]

180 Days of PROBLEM SOLVING
for Fifth Grade

- ❓ Think
- 🔑 Plan
- 💡 Solve
- 🔍 Explain

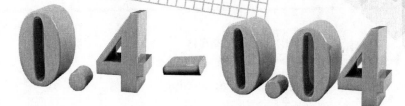

0.4 - 0.04

Author
Stacy Monsman, M.A.

SHELL EDUCATION

For information on how this resource meets national and other state standards, see pages 4–7. You may also review this information by visiting our website at www.teachercreatedmaterials.com/administrators/correlations/ and following the on-screen directions.

Publishing Credits

Corinne Burton, M.A.Ed., *Publisher*; Conni Medina, M.A.Ed., *Managing Editor*; Emily R. Smith, M.A.Ed., *Series Developer*; Diana Kenney, M.A.Ed., NBCT, *Content Director*; Paula Makridis, M.A.Ed., *Editor*; Lee Aucoin, *Multimedia Designer*; Kyleena Harper, *Assistant Editor*; Kevin Pham, *Graphic Designer*

Image Credits

All images from iStock and Shutterstock.

Standards

Shell Education

A division of Teacher Created Materials
5301 Oceanus Drive
Huntington Beach, CA 92649-1030

www.tcmpub.com/shell-education
ISBN 978-1-4258-1617-9
©2017 Shell Education Publishing, Inc.

TABLE OF CONTENTS

INTRODUCTION

The Need for Practice

To be successful in today's mathematics classrooms, students must deeply understand both concepts and procedures so that they can discuss and demonstrate their understanding during the problem-solving process. Demonstrating understanding is a process that must be continually practiced for students to be successful. Practice is especially important to help students apply their concrete, conceptual understanding during each step of the problem-solving process.

Understanding Assessment

In addition to providing opportunities for frequent practice, teachers must be able to assess students' problem-solving skills. This is important so that teachers can adequately address students' misconceptions, build on their current understandings, and challenge them appropriately. Assessment is a long-term process that involves careful analysis of student responses from discussions, projects, practice pages, or tests. When analyzing the data, it is important for teachers to reflect on how their teaching practices may have influenced students' responses and to identify those areas where additional instruction may be required. In short, the data gathered from assessments should be used to inform instruction: slow down, speed up, or reteach. This type of assessment is called *formative assessment*.

HOW TO USE THIS BOOK

180 Days of Problem Solving offers teachers and parents problem-solving activities for each day of the school year. Students will build their problem-solving skills as they develop a deeper understanding of mathematical concepts and apply these concepts to real-life situations. This series will also help students improve their critical-thinking and reasoning skills, use visual models when solving problems, approach problems in multiple ways, and solve multi-step, non-routine word problems.

Easy-to-Use and Standards-Based

These daily activities reinforce grade-level skills across a variety of mathematical concepts. Each day provides a full practice page, making the activities easy to prepare and implement as part of a classroom routine, at the beginning of each mathematics lesson as a warm-up or Problem of the Day, or as homework. Students can work on the practice pages independently or in cooperative groups. The practice pages can also be utilized as diagnostic tools, formative assessments, or summative assessments, which can direct differentiated small-group instruction during Mathematics Workshop.

Domains and Practice Standards

The chart below indicates the mathematics domains addressed and practice standards applied throughout this book. The subsequent chart shows the breakdown of which mathematics standard is covered in each week.

Note: Students may not have a deep understanding of some topics in this book. Remember to assess students based on their problem-solving skills and not exclusively on their content knowledge.

Grade-Level Domains	Standards of Mathematical Practice
1. Operations and Algebraic Thinking	1. Make sense of problems and persevere in solving them.
2. Number and Operations in Base Ten	2. Reason abstractly and quantitatively.
3. Number and Operations—Fractions	3. Construct viable arguments and critique the reasoning of others.
4. Measurement and Data	4. Model with mathematics.
5. Geometry	5. Use appropriate tools strategically.
	6. Attend to precision.
	7. Look for and make use of structure.
	8. Look for and express regularity in repeated reasoning.

HOW TO USE THIS BOOK *(cont.)*

College-and-Career Readiness Standards

Below is a list of mathematical standards that are addressed throughout this book. Each week, students solve problems related to the same mathematical topic.

Week	Standard
1	Explain patterns in the number of zeros of the product when multiplying a number by powers of 10, and explain patterns in the placement of the decimal point when a decimal is multiplied or divided by a power of 10. Use whole-number exponents to denote powers of 10.
2	Use parentheses, brackets, or braces in numerical expressions, and evaluate expressions with these symbols.
3	Write simple expressions that record calculations with numbers, and interpret numerical expressions without evaluating them.
4	Fluently multiply multi-digit whole numbers using the standard algorithm.
5	Find whole-number quotients of whole numbers with up to four-digit dividends and two-digit divisors, using strategies based on place value, the properties of operations, and/or the relationship between multiplication and division. Illustrate and explain the calculation by using equations, rectangular arrays, and/or area models.
6	Recognize volume as an attribute of solid figures and understand concepts of volume measurement.
7	Measure volumes by counting unit cubes, using cubic cm, cubic in., cubic ft., and improvised units.
8	Relate volume to the operations of multiplication and addition and solve real world and mathematical problems involving volume.
9	Add fractions with unlike denominators (including mixed numbers) by replacing given fractions with equivalent fractions in such a way as to produce an equivalent sum or difference of fractions with like denominators.
10	Subtract fractions with unlike denominators (including mixed numbers) by replacing given fractions with equivalent fractions in such a way as to produce an equivalent sum or difference of fractions with like denominators.
11	Solve word problems involving addition and subtraction of fractions referring to the same whole, including cases of unlike denominators (e.g., by using visual fraction models or equations to represent the problem).
12	Interpret a fraction as division of the numerator by the denominator ($\frac{a}{b} = a \div b$). Solve word problems involving division of whole numbers leading to answers in the form of fractions or mixed numbers (e.g., by using visual fraction models or equations to represent the problem).

13	Apply and extend previous understandings of multiplication to multiply a whole number by a fraction.
14	Apply and extend previous understandings of multiplication to multiply a fraction by a fraction.
15	Compare the size of a product to the size of one factor on the basis of the size of the other factor, without performing the indicated multiplication.
16	Solve real world problems involving multiplication of fractions and mixed numbers (e.g., by using visual fraction models or equations to represent the problem).
17	Apply and extend previous understandings of division to divide whole numbers by unit fractions.
18	Apply and extend previous understandings of division to divide unit fractions by whole numbers.
19	Solve real-world problems involving division of unit fractions by non-zero whole numbers and division of whole numbers by unit fractions (e.g., by using visual fraction models and equations to represent the problem).
20	Convert among different-sized standard measurement units within a given measurement system (e.g., convert 5 cm to 0.05 m), and use these conversions in solving multi-step, real-world problems.
21	Make a line plot to display a data set of measurements in fractions of a unit ($\frac{1}{2}$, $\frac{1}{4}$, $\frac{1}{8}$). Use operations on fractions for this grade to solve problems involving information presented in line plots.
22	Recognize that in a multi-digit number, a digit in one place represents 10 times as much as it represents in the place to its right and $\frac{1}{10}$ of what it represents in the place to its left.
23	Explain patterns in the number of zeros of the product when multiplying a number by powers of 10, and explain patterns in the placement of the decimal point when a decimal is multiplied or divided by a power of 10. Use whole-number exponents to denote powers of 10.
24	Read and write decimals to thousandths using base-ten numerals, number names, and expanded form.
25	Compare two decimals to thousandths based on meanings of the digits in each place, using >, =, and < symbols to record the results of comparisons.
26	Use place value understanding to round decimals to any place.
27	Add decimals to hundredths, using concrete models or drawings and strategies based on place value, properties of operations, and/or the relationship between addition and subtraction; relate the strategy to a written method and explain the reasoning used.

HOW TO USE THIS BOOK (cont.)

28	Subtract decimals to hundredths, using concrete models or drawings and strategies based on place value, properties of operations, and/or the relationship between addition and subtraction; relate the strategy to a written method and explain the reasoning used.
29	Multiply decimals to hundredths, using concrete models or drawings and strategies based on place value, properties of operations, and/or the relationship between addition and subtraction; relate the strategy to a written method and explain the reasoning used.
30	Divide decimals to hundredths, using contcrete models or drawings and strategies based on place value, properties of operations, and/or the relationship between addition and subtraction; relate the strategy to a written method and explain the reasoning used.
31	Convert among different-sized standard measurement units within a given measurement system (e.g., convert 5 cm to 0.05 m), and use these conversions in solving multi-step, real-world problems.
32	Understand that attributes belonging to a category of two-dimensional figures also belong to all subcategories of that category.
33	Classify two-dimensional figures in a hierarchy based on properties.
34	Generate two numerical patterns using two given rules. Identify apparent relationships between corresponding terms. Form ordered pairs consisting of corresponding terms from the two patterns, and graph the ordered pairs on a coordinate plane.
35	Use a pair of perpendicular number lines, called axes, to define a coordinate system, with the intersection of the lines (the origin) arranged to coincide with the 0 on each line and a given point in the plane located by using an ordered pair of numbers, called its coordinates. Understand that the first number indicates how far to travel from the origin in the direction of one axis, and the second number indicates how far to travel in the direction of the second axis, with the convention that the names of the two axes and the coordinates correspond (e.g., x-axis and x-coordinate, y-axis and y-coordinate).
36	Represent real world and mathematical problems by graphing points in the first quadrant of the coordinate plane, and interpret coordinate values of points in the context of the situation.

HOW TO USE THIS BOOK *(cont.)*

Using the Practice Pages

The activity pages provide practice and assessment opportunities for each day of the school year. Students focus on one grade-level skill each week. The five-day plan requires students to think about the problem-solving process, use visual models, choose multiple strategies, and solve multi-step, non-routine word problems. For this grade level, students may complete the pages independently or in cooperative groups. Teachers may prepare packets of weekly practice pages for the classroom or for homework.

Day 1–Think About It!

For the first day of each week, the focus is on thinking about the problem-solving process. Students might draw pictures or answer questions about a problem. The goal is to understand the process of solving a problem more so than finding the solution.

Day 2–Solve It!

On the second day of each week, students solve one to two routine problems based on the thinking process from Day 1. Students think about the information given in the problem, decide on a plan, solve the problem, and look back and explain their work.

Day 3–Visualize It!

On day three, a visual representation (e.g., number line, table, diagram, fraction model) is shown as a strategy for solving a problem. Students use this visual model to solve a similar problem.

Day 4–Solve It Two Ways!

On the fourth day, students solve the same problem two ways by applying the strategies they have learned. Students may also be asked to analyze how others solved a problem and explain which way is correct or state the error or misconception.

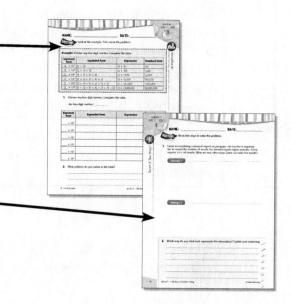

HOW TO USE THIS BOOK *(cont.)*

Day 5–Challenge Yourself!
On day five, students are presented with a multi-step, non-routine problem. Students analyze a problem, think about different strategies, develop a plan, and explain how they solved the problem.

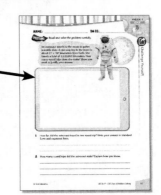

Using the Resources

The following resources will be helpful to students as they complete the activity pages. Print copies of these resources and provide them to students to keep at their desks. These resources are available as Adobe® PDFs online. A complete list of the available documents is provided on page 222. To access the digital resources, go to this website: **http://www.tcmpub.com/download-files**. Enter this code: 55497002. Follow the on-screen directions.

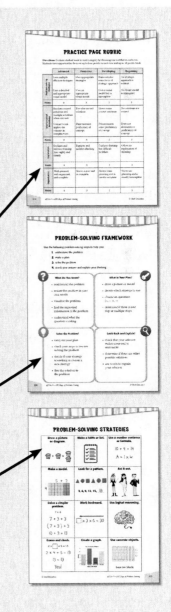

Practice Page Rubric can be found on page 214 and in the Digital Resources (rubric.pdf). The rubric can be used to assess students' mathematical understanding of the weekly concept and steps in the problem-solving process. The rubric should be shared with students so they know what is expected of them.

Problem-Solving Framework can be found on page 220 and in the Digital Resources (framework.pdf). Students can reference each step of the problem-solving process as they complete the practice pages during the week.

Problem-Solving Strategies can be found on page 221 and in the Digital Resources (strategies.pdf). Students may want to reference this page when choosing strategies as they solve problems throughout the week.

HOW TO USE THIS BOOK *(cont.)*

Diagnostic Assessment

Teachers can use the practice pages as diagnostic assessments. The data analysis tools included with the book enable teachers or parents to quickly score students' work and monitor their progress. Teachers and parents can quickly see which steps in the problem-solving process students need to target further to develop proficiency.

After students complete a week of practice pages, each page can be graded using the answer key (pages 193–213). Then, the *Practice Page Rubric* (page 214; rubric.pdf) can be used to score each practice page. The *Practice Page Item Analysis* (pages 215–218; itemanalysis.pdf) can be completed. The *Practice Page Item Analysis* can be used to record students' Day 5 practice page score, while the *Student Item Analysis* (page 219; studentitem.pdf) can be used to record a student's daily practice page score. These charts are also provided in the Digital Resources as PDFs, Microsoft Word® files (itemanalysis.docx; studentitem.docx), and Microsoft Excel® files (itemanalysis.xlsx; studentitem.xlsx). Teachers can input data into the electronic files directly on the computer, or they can print the pages and analyze students' work using paper and pencil.

To Complete the Practice Page Item Analysis

- Write or type students' names in the far-left column. Depending on the number of students, more than one copy of the form may be needed, or you may need to add rows.

- The specific week is indicated across the top of each chart.

- Record rubric scores for the Day 5 practice page in the appropriate column.

- Add the scores for each student. Place that sum in the far-right column. Use these scores as benchmarks to determine how each student is performing after a nine-week period. This allows for four benchmarks during the year that can be used to gather formative diagnostic data.

HOW TO USE THIS BOOK (cont.)

To Complete the Student Item Analysis

- Write or type the student's name in the top row. This form tracks the ongoing process of each student, so one copy per student is necessary.

- The specific day is indicated across the top of each chart.

- Record the student's rubric score for each practice page in the appropriate column.

- Add the scores for the student. Place that sum in the far-right column. Use these scores as benchmarks to determine how the student is performing each week. These benchmarks can be used to gather formative diagnostic data.

Using the Results to Differentiate Instruction

Once results are gathered and analyzed, teachers can use the results to inform the way they differentiate instruction. The data can help determine which mathematical concepts and steps in the problem-solving process are the most difficult for students and which students need additional instructional support and continued practice.

Whole-Class Support

The results of the diagnostic analysis may show that the entire class is struggling with a particular mathematical concept or problem-solving step. If these concepts or problem-solving steps have been taught in the past, this indicates that further instruction or reteaching is necessary. If these concepts or steps have not been taught in the past, this data is a great preassessment and may demonstrate that students do not have a working knowledge of the concepts or steps. Thus, careful planning for the length of the unit(s) or lesson(s) must be considered, and additional front-loading may be required.

Small-Group or Individual Support

The results of the diagnostic analysis may show that an individual student or small group of students is struggling with a particular mathematical concept or problem-solving step. If these concepts or steps have been taught in the past, this indicates that further instruction or reteaching is necessary. These students can be pulled to a small group for further instruction on the concept(s) or step(s), while other students work independently. Students may also benefit from extra practice using games or computer-based resources. Teachers can also use the results to help identify individual students or groups of proficient students who are ready for enrichment or above-grade-level instruction. These groups may benefit from independent learning contracts or more challenging activities.

Digital Resources

The Digital Resources contain digital copies of activity pages, diagnostic pages, and additional resources, such as the *Problem-Solving Framework* and *Problem-Solving Strategies* pages, for students. The list of resources in the Digital Resources can be found on page 222.

STANDARDS CORRELATIONS

Shell Education is committed to producing educational materials that are research- and standards-based. In this effort, we have correlated all of our products to the academic standards of all 50 states, the District of Columbia, the Department of Defense Dependents Schools, and all Canadian provinces.

How to Find Standards Correlations

To print a customized correlation report of this product for your state, visit our website at **http://www.tcmpub.com/shell-education**. If you require assistance in printing correlation reports, please contact our Customer Service Department at 1-877-777-3450.

Purpose and Intent of Standards

The Every Student Succeeds Act (ESSA) mandates that all states adopt challenging academic standards that help students meet the goal of college and career readiness. While many states already adopted academic standards prior to ESSA, the act continues to hold states accountable for detailed and comprehensive standards.

Standards are designed to focus instruction and guide adoption of curricula. Standards are statements that describe the criteria necessary for students to meet specific academic goals. They define the knowledge, skills, and content students should acquire at each level. Standards are also used to develop standardized tests to evaluate students' academic progress.

Teachers are required to demonstrate how their lessons meet state standards. State standards are used in the development of all of our products, so educators can be assured they meet the academic requirements of each state.

The activities in this book are aligned to today's national and state-specific college-and-career readiness standards. The chart on page 4 lists the domains and practice standards addressed throughout this book. A more detailed chart on pages 5–7 correlates the specific mathematics content standards to each week.

NAME: _____   **DATE:** _____

 DIRECTIONS: Think about the problem, and answer the questions.

Max likes to practice math with his sister, Marsha. She writes a problem for him with blanks given for the solution. There is one blank for each digit in the solution. Marsha gives Max this problem:

$38 \times 10^5 =$ _____ _____ _____ _____ _____ _____ _____

1. Why does Marsha write 7 blanks for the solution? Explain how you know.

_____

_____

_____

2. If the problem was 38×10^4, would that change the number of blanks Marsha writes for Max? Why or why not?

_____

_____

_____

3. If the problem was 3×10^5, how many blanks would Marsha need to write for Max? How do you know?

_____

_____

_____

Solve It!

NAME: _____ **DATE:** _____

DIRECTIONS: Read and solve each problem.

Problem 1: Max likes to practice math with his sister, Marsha. She writes a problem for him with blanks given for the solution. There is one blank for each digit in the solution. Marsha gives Max this problem:

$$38 \times 10^5 = \underline{\quad}\ \underline{\quad}\ \underline{\quad}\ \underline{\quad}\ \underline{\quad}\ \underline{\quad}\ \underline{\quad}$$

 What Do You Know?

 What Is Your Plan?

 Solve the Problem!

 Look Back and Explain!

Problem 2: Max wants Marsha to write a second problem for him. Marsha gives him this problem:

$$3 \times 10^4 = \underline{\quad}\ \underline{\quad}\ \underline{\quad}\ \underline{\quad}\ \underline{\quad}$$

 What Do You Know?

 What Is Your Plan?

 Solve the Problem!

 Look Back and Explain!

NAME: _____ DATE: _____

 DIRECTIONS: Look at the example. Then, solve the problem.

Example: Choose any two-digit number. Complete the table.

Exponent form	Expanded form	Expression	Standard form
12 × 10¹	12 × 10	12 × 10	120
12 × 10²	12 × 10 × 10	12 × 100	1,200
12 × 10³	12 × 10 × 10 × 10	12 × 1,000	12,000
12 × 10⁴	12 × 10 × 10 × 10 × 10	12 × 10,000	120,000
12 × 10⁵	12 × 10 × 10 × 10 × 10 × 10	12 × 100,000	1,200,000
12 × 10⁶	12 × 10 × 10 × 10 × 10 × 10 × 10	12 × 1,000,000	12,000,000

1. Choose any two-digit number. Complete the table.

My two-digit number: _____ _____

Exponent form	Expanded form	Expression	Standard form
_____ × 10¹			
_____ × 10²			
_____ × 10³			
_____ × 10⁴			
_____ × 10⁵			
_____ × 10⁶			

2. What patterns do you notice in the table?

_____

_____

_____

Solve It Two Ways!

NAME: _____ **DATE:** _____

 **DIRECTIONS:** Show two ways to solve the problem.

1. Carrie is completing a research report on penguins. Her teacher is requiring her to record the number of results the Internet search engine provides. Carrie reports 14×10^6 results. What are two other ways Carrie can write her results?

Strategy 1

Strategy 2

2. Which way do you think best represents the information? Explain your reasoning.

_____

_____

_____

_____

_____

NAME: _____ **DATE:** _____

DIRECTIONS: Read and solve the problem.

An astronaut travels to the moon to gather scientific data. A one-way trip to the moon is about 37×10^4 kilometers from Earth. She travels a total of 2,220,000 kilometers. How many round trips does she make? Show your work to justify your answer.

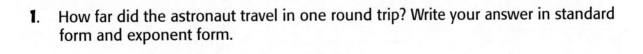

1. How far did the astronaut travel in one round trip? Write your answer in standard form and exponent form.

_____

_____

2. How many round trips did the astronaut make? Explain how you know.

_____

_____

_____

_____

Think About It!

NAME: _____ **DATE:** _____

DIRECTIONS: Think about the problem, and answer the questions.

Mrs. Johnson writes some math problems on the board. She writes the first problem as $15 \times (12 + 8)$. Katy copies the problem quickly into her notebook and writes $15 \times 12 + 8$. Will Katy get the answer her teacher is expecting? Why or why not?

1. What is the first step in the teacher's problem? How do you know?

_____

_____

_____

2. What is the first step in the problem Katy wrote? How do you know?

_____

_____

_____

3. Do you think the two problems will result in the same answer? Why or why not?

_____

_____

_____

#51617—180 Days of Problem Solving

NAME: _____ **DATE:** _____

 DIRECTIONS: Read and solve each problem.

Problem 1: Mrs. Johnson writes some math problems on the board. She writes the first problem as 15 × (12 + 8). Katy copies the problem quickly into her notebook and writes 15 × 12 + 8. Will Katy get the answer her teacher is expecting? Why or why not?

 What Do You Know?

 What Is Your Plan?

 Solve the Problem!

 Look Back and Explain!

Problem 2: Mrs. Johnson writes a second problem as 95 − 20 + 8. Katy writes 95 − (20 + 8). Will Katy get the answer her teacher is expecting? Why or why not?

 What Do You Know?

 What Is Your Plan?

 Solve the Problem!

 Look Back and Explain!

Visualize It!

NAME: _____ **DATE:** _____

DIRECTIONS: Look at the example. Then, solve the problem.

Example: Evaluate the expression without grouping symbols. Then, evaluate the expression with grouping symbols.

Expression with no grouping symbols	Expression with grouping symbols
$2 \times 4 \times 6 + 3 \times 15 - 12 + 10^2$	$2 \times \{4 \times [6 + 3 \times (15 - 12)] + 10^2\}$
$2 \times 4 \times 6 + 3 \times 15 - 12 + 100$	$2 \times \{4 \times [6 + 3 \times 3] + 10^2\}$
$48 + 45 - 12 + 100$	$2 \times \{4 \times [6 + 9] + 10^2\}$
$93 - 12 + 100$	$2 \times \{4 \times 15 + 10^2\}$
$81 + 100$	$2 \times \{60 + 10^2\}$
181	$2 \times \{60 + 100\}$
	2×160
	320

1. Evaluate the expression without grouping symbols. Then, evaluate the expression with grouping symbols.

Expression with no grouping symbols	Expression with grouping symbols
$5 \times 2 \times 6 - 3 \times 4 + 8 + 10^3$	$5 \times \{2 \times [(6 - 3) \times 4 + 8]\} + 10^3$

2. Did you get the same answer for both expressions? Why or why not?

_____

_____

NAME: _____ **DATE:** _____

 DIRECTIONS: Show two ways to solve the problem.

1. Place grouping symbols in the equations to make true statements.

········ Strategy 1 ···

$$5 + 4 \times 9 \div 3 + 7 = 34$$

········ Strategy 2 ···

$$5 + 4 \times 9 \div 3 + 7 = 45$$

2. Describe your strategies for solving the problems. Did your strategy work the first time you tried it? What did you do to change your strategy?

_____

_____

_____

_____

_____

Challenge Yourself!

NAME: _____ **DATE:** _____

DIRECTIONS: Read and solve the problem.

Find five different equations having a solution of 10 by following these rules:

- Use the numbers 1, 2, 3, and 4 in any order exactly once in each equation.
- Use any combination of grouping symbols.
- Use any combination of addition, subtraction, multiplication, and division.

1. Write five equations using the rules given.

_____

_____

_____

_____

_____

2. How did you determine where to put grouping symbols?

_____

_____

_____

NAME: _____ DATE: _____

DIRECTIONS: Think about the problem, and answer the questions.

Compare the expressions. How are the two expressions related?

$$5 \times 7 \qquad 10(5 \times 7)$$

Think About It!

1. Use words to describe the first expression.

_____

_____

_____

_____

2. Use words to describe the second expression.

_____

_____

_____

_____

3. Which expression will have a greater solution? How do you know?

_____

_____

_____

_____

NAME: _____ **DATE:** _____

DIRECTIONS: Read and solve each problem.

Solve It!

Problem 1: Compare the expressions. How are the two expressions related?

$$5 \times 7 \qquad\qquad 10(5 \times 7)$$

 What Do You Know?

 What Is Your Plan?

 Solve the Problem!

 Look Back and Explain!

Problem 2: Compare the expressions. How are the two expressions related?

$$120 + 25 \qquad\qquad 3 \times (120 + 25)$$

 What Do You Know?

 What Is Your Plan?

 Solve the Problem!

 Look Back and Explain!

NAME: _____ **DATE:** _____

DIRECTIONS: Look at the example. Then, solve the problem.

Example: Write the missing descriptions and expressions.

Description	Expression
Add 6 and 7. Multiply the result by 9.	$9(6 + 7)$
Double 22 and then subtract 4.	$(2 \times 22) - 4$
Subtract 3 from 18. Divide the difference by 5.	$(18 - 3) \div 5$
Combine 35 and 12. Subtract 7. Then, multiply that result by 11.	$11(35 + 12 - 7)$

1. Write the missing descriptions and expressions.

Description	Expression
Triple 18 and add 12.	
	$45 \div 5 - 2$
	$6(72 \div 8)$
Find the sum of 21 and 15. Find the quotient of the sum and 3.	

2. Other than *add, subtract, multiply,* and *divide,* which words in the descriptions tell you how to write the expressions?

_____

_____

_____

_____

Solve It Two Ways!

NAME: _____ **DATE:** _____

DIRECTIONS: Show two ways to solve the problem.

1. Compare the descriptions and expressions. Are both expressions correct ways to represent the description? Why or why not?

Strategy 1

Description: Double 10 and add 14.

Possible Expressions: (2 × 10) + 14   14 + (2 × 10)

_____

_____

_____

Strategy 2

Description: Double 10 and subtract 14.

Possible Expressions: (2 × 10) – 14   14 – (2 × 10)

_____

_____

_____

2. When does the order of the numbers and operation signs matter when writing an expression?

_____

_____

_____

_____

_____

NAME: _____ **DATE:** _____

DIRECTIONS: Read and solve the problem.

Alejandro is playing a math game on his tablet. In round 1, he scores 500 points. He earns 750 additional points in round 2. Then, he loses 200 points for an incorrect answer in round 3. Finally, Alejandro answers a bonus question that triples his points. Write an expression that represents Alejandro's total score.

1. What is one way you can write an expression for Alejandro's total score?

_____

2. Is there a different way you can represent Alejandro's total score? Show your thinking.

_____

3. Pretend Alejandro plays the game a second time. Write the number of points he earns or loses for three rounds. Then, write an expression for his total score in two different ways.

Round	Points
1	
2	
3	

Expression 1:

_____

Expression 2:

_____

Think About It!

NAME: _____ **DATE:** _____

 **DIRECTIONS:** Think about the problem, and answer the questions.

> A bookstore orders
> 175 dozen pencils.
> How many pencils
> are there in all?

1. What information is given?

_____

_____

2. What strategy can you use to solve the problem?

_____

_____

_____

3. Can you think of a different way to show the problem? Explain your thinking.

_____

_____

_____

_____

#51617—180 Days of Problem Solving © Shell Education

NAME: _____ **DATE:** _____

 DIRECTIONS: Read and solve each problem.

Problem 1: A bookstore orders 175 dozen pencils. How many pencils are there in all?

? What Do You Know?

🔑 What Is Your Plan?

💡 Solve the Problem!

🔍 Look Back and Explain!

Problem 2: The bookstore also orders 36 packages of erasers. The erasers come in packs of 25. How many erasers are there in all?

? What Do You Know?

🔑 What Is Your Plan?

💡 Solve the Problem!

🔍 Look Back and Explain!

WEEK 4 — DAY 3

Visualize It!

NAME: _____ **DATE:** _____

DIRECTIONS: Look at the example. Then, solve the problem.

Example:
286 × 42

×	200	80	6
40	8,000	3,200	240
2	400	160	12

8,000 + 3,200 + 240 + 400 + 160 + 12 = 12,012

1. 537 × 89

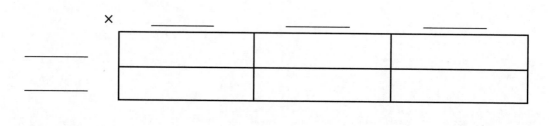

_____ + _____ + _____ + _____ + _____ + _____ = _____

2. How does the model help you solve the problem?

_____

_____

_____

_____

_____

_____

_____

_____

_____

30   #51617—180 Days of Problem Solving   © Shell Education

NAME: _____ **DATE:** _____

DIRECTIONS: Show two ways to solve the problem.

1. Scott's school is selling bags of microwave popcorn for a fundraiser. The popcorn comes in boxes of 24 bags. They sell 358 boxes. How many bags of popcorn did they sell?

Strategy 1

Strategy 2

2. Which strategy do you think is better? Explain your reasoning.

_____

_____

_____

_____

Challenge Yourself!

NAME: _____ **DATE:** _____

DIRECTIONS: Read and solve the problem.

Yoshi needs to make the greatest possible product using the digits 5 through 9. He can only use each number one time. What is the greatest product Yoshi can make?

1. Write the expression that will produce the greatest product.

_____ × _____

2. Explain why your expression will produce the greatest product.

_____

_____

NAME: _____ DATE: _____

 DIRECTIONS: Think about the problem, and answer the questions.

Central Middle School needs to put students into groups of 14 for their upcoming field days. There are 1,572 students at the school. How many groups will there be? Will there be any students left over?

1. What information is given?

    _____

    _____

    _____

    _____

    _____

    _____

2. Will there be less than or more than 100 groups for the field days? How do you know?

    _____

    _____

    _____

    _____

    _____

NAME: _____ **DATE:** _____

Solve It!

DIRECTIONS: Read and solve each problem.

Problem 1: Central Middle School needs to put students into groups of 14 for their upcoming field days. There are 1,572 students at the school. How many groups will there be? Will there be any students left over?

 What Do You Know?

 What Is Your Plan?

 Solve the Problem!

 Look Back and Explain!

Problem 2: North Middle School is putting their students in groups of 8 for their upcoming field days. There are 936 students at the school. How many groups will there be? Will there be any students left over?

 What Do You Know?

 What Is Your Plan?

 Solve the Problem!

 Look Back and Explain!

NAME: _____ DATE: _____

DIRECTIONS: Look at the example. Then, solve the problem.

Visualize It!

Example: 4,728 ÷ 21

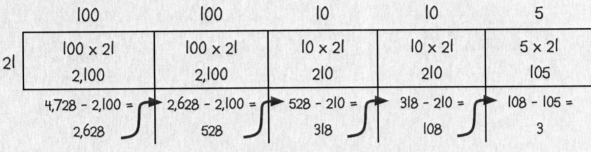

$$100 + 100 + 10 + 10 + 5 = 225$$

$$4,728 ÷ 21 = 225, \text{ remainder } 3$$

1. 8,227 ÷ 72

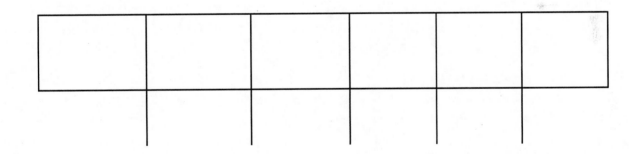

_____ = _____

8,227 ÷ 72 = _____

2. How does the model help you solve the problem?

_____

_____

_____

Solve It Two Ways!

NAME: _____ **DATE:** _____

DIRECTIONS: Show two ways to solve the problem.

1. Maya needs to distribute 7,632 packages of paper to 36 classrooms. How many packages of paper will each classroom receive?

Strategy 1

Strategy 2

2. Which strategy do you like better? Explain your reasoning.

_____

_____

_____

_____

_____

NAME: _____ DATE: _____

  Read and solve the problem.

Breanna's entire office is moving to a new location. She is helping to fill two moving vans with boxes. The small van can hold up to 15 boxes. The large van can hold up to 25 boxes. There are 800 boxes that must be moved. How many trips will the two vans need to take to transport all of the boxes to the new location?

1. Show your plan for transporting all of the boxes.

2. Is there another way to transport all of the boxes? Explain your thinking.

_____

_____

_____

3. Which plan do you think is better? Explain your reasoning.

_____

_____

_____

Think About It!

NAME: _____ DATE: _____

DIRECTIONS: Think about the problem, and answer the questions.

Amy says, "I see 2 layers of 12 unit cubes." Janet says, "I see 2 layers of 8 unit cubes." Who is correct?

1. How many layers of cubes does the figure have? _____

2. How many cubes are in each layer? _____

3. What can you do to find the volume of the figure?

_____

_____

_____

_____

_____

NAME: _____ **DATE:** _____

DIRECTIONS: Read and solve each problem.

Problem 1: Amy says, "I see 2 layers of 12 unit cubes." Janet says, "I see 2 layers of 8 unit cubes." Who is correct?

? What Do You Know?

🔑 What Is Your Plan?

💡 Solve the Problem!

🔍 Look Back and Explain!

Problem 2: Hector says, "I see 5 layers of 8 unit cubes." Jesse says, "I see 2 layers of 10 unit cubes." Who is correct?

? What Do You Know?

🔑 What Is Your Plan?

💡 Solve the Problem!

🔍 Look Back and Explain!

Visualize It!

NAME: _____ DATE: _____

DIRECTIONS: Look at the example. Then, solve the problem.

Example: Find the total number of unit cubes in the figure.

Figure	Base layer	Number of layers	Total number of unit cubes
	__9__ cubic units	3	27

1. Find the total number of unit cubes in the figure.

Figure	Base layer	Number of layers	Total number of unit cubes
	_____ cubic units		

2. How does knowing the number of layers and the number of unit cubes in each layer help you find the total number of unit cubes?

_____

_____

_____

_____

_____

_____

NAME: _____ DATE: _____

 DIRECTIONS: Show two ways to solve the problem.

1. Rachael packages caramels at a candy store. Each caramel is 1 cubic inch. A small box must include 8 caramels. Rachael has to design a box in the shape of a rectangular prism or a cube that will hold exactly that amount. Design two boxes Rachael can use to package the caramels.

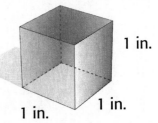

1 in.

1 in.

1 in.

Strategy 1

Strategy 2

2. Which package do you recommend the candy store use? Explain your reasoning.

_____

_____

_____

_____

_____

Solve It Two Ways!

Challenge Yourself!

NAME: _____ DATE: _____

DIRECTIONS: Read and solve the problem.

A sporting goods company packages basketballs in small boxes that are 1 cubic foot. Design four different boxes in the shape of a rectangular prism or a cube that can be used to ship 24 basketballs. Be sure to prove that each design holds 24 cubic feet.

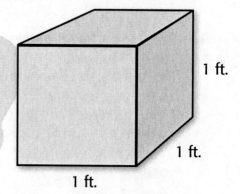

1 ft.

1 ft.

1 ft.

1. Sketch each design, and show how each holds 24 cubic feet.

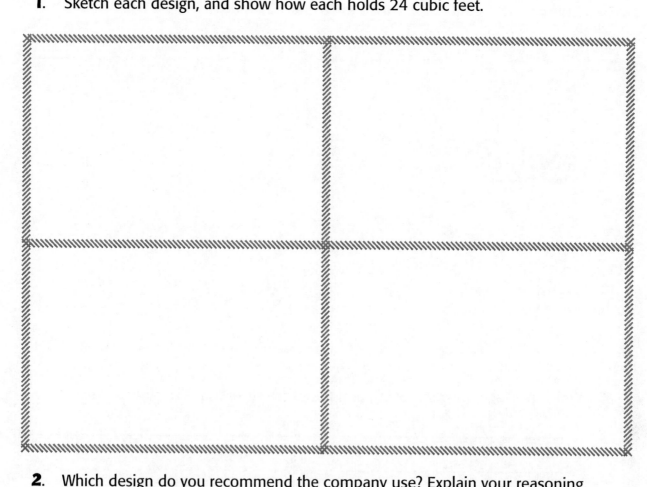

2. Which design do you recommend the company use? Explain your reasoning.

_____

_____

_____

NAME: _____ **DATE:** _____

DIRECTIONS: Think about the problem, and answer the questions.

Jamila has a gift box that is 8 centimeters long, 8 centimeters wide, and 2 centimeters high. It has a volume of 128 cubic centimeters. She has a second gift box that is the same width but is twice the length and three times the height. What is the volume of the second gift box?

Think About It!

1. What information is given?

_____

_____

_____

2. What is the question asking you to find?

_____

_____

_____

3. Can the answer be 128 cubic centimeters? Why or why not?

_____

_____

_____

_____

NAME: _____ **DATE:** _____

Solve It!

DIRECTIONS: Read and solve each problem.

Problem 1: Jamila has a gift box that is 8 centimeters long, 8 centimeters wide, and 2 centimeters high. It has a volume of 128 cubic centimeters. She has a second gift box that is the same width but is twice the length and three times the height. What is the volume of the second gift box?

 What Do You Know?

 What Is Your Plan?

 Solve the Problem!

 Look Back and Explain!

Problem 2: Tonya has a tool chest that is 5 feet long, 3 feet wide, and 4 feet high. It has a volume of 60 cubic feet. She has a second tool chest that has the same width, twice the length, and half the height. What is the volume of the second tool chest?

What Do You Know?

What Is Your Plan?

 Solve the Problem!

 Look Back and Explain!

NAME: _____ DATE: _____

 DIRECTIONS: Look at the example. Then, solve the problem.

Example: Sketch the figure and find the volume.

Sketch	Dimensions length × width × height	Volume
3 ⬚ 2 4	4 × 2 × 3	24 cubic units

1. Sketch each figure and find the volume.

Sketch	Dimensions length × width × height	Volume
	2 × 3 × 4	
	3 × 4 × 2	

2. Does the order of the dimensions change the volume? Why or why not?

_____

_____

_____

Solve It Two Ways!

NAME: _____ **DATE:** _____

DIRECTIONS: Show two ways to solve the problem.

1. Mrs. Clark is sending a care package to her daughter who is away at college. She needs a box that holds 36 cubic inches. Sketch two different boxes that Mrs. Clark can use to send her package. Write an equation for each sketch to justify your reasoning.

Strategy 1 ·

Strategy 2 ·

2. Do you think there are more than two solutions to this problem? Why or why not?

_____

_____

_____

_____

_____

NAME: _____ **DATE:** _____

DIRECTIONS: Read and solve the problem.

Alex has a bird feeder that has a height of 30 centimeters, length of 10 centimeters, and width of 8 centimeters. His friend has a bird feeder that has twice the volume. What could be the possible height, length, and width of his friend's bird feeder?

1. Write an equation to find the volume of Alex's bird feeder.

   _____

2. Sketch Alex's friend's bird feeder and label the length, width, and height. Show how you found your solution.

3. Can you think of a different way to sketch his friend's bird feeder? Explain your thinking.

   _____

   _____

   _____

Think About It!

NAME: _____ DATE: _____

DIRECTIONS: Think about the problem, and answer the questions.

Find the volume of the figure.

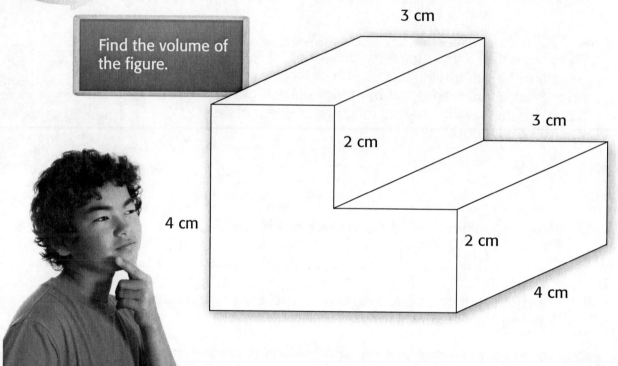

3 cm

2 cm

3 cm

4 cm

2 cm

4 cm

1. Will multiplying all of the given side lengths result in the correct volume of the figure? Why or why not?

_____

_____

_____

_____

2. Find two rectangular prisms that make up the figure. Shade each of the two prisms you see in different colors. What are their dimensions?

_____

_____

_____

_____

NAME: _____ **DATE:** _____

 DIRECTIONS: Read and solve each problem.

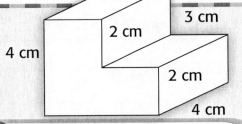

Problem 1: Find the volume of the figure.

3 cm

3 cm

2 cm

4 cm

2 cm

2 cm

4 cm

? What Do You Know?

🔑 What Is Your Plan?

💡 Solve the Problem!

🔍 Look Back and Explain!

Problem 2: Find the volume of the figure.

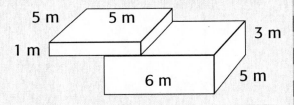

5 m   5 m

1 m   3 m

6 m   5 m

? What Do You Know?

🔑 What Is Your Plan?

💡 Solve the Problem!

🔍 Look Back and Explain!

Solve It!

© Shell Education

NAME: _____ DATE: _____

DIRECTIONS: Look at the example. Then, solve the problem.

Example: Find the volume of the figure.

Figure	Prism 1 dimensions and volume	Prism 2 dimensions and volume	Total volume
4 ft. 2 ft. 2 ft. 1 ft. 5 ft.	$1 \times 2 \times 4 =$ 8 cubic feet	$5 \times 2 \times 2 =$ 20 cubic feet	$8 + 20 =$ 28 cubic feet

1. Find the volume of the figure.

Figure	Prism 1 dimensions and volume	Prism 2 dimensions and volume	Total volume
1 ft. 2 ft. 6 ft. 3 ft. 8 ft. 3 ft.			

2. Explain how you found the total volume of the figure.

_____

_____

_____

_____

NAME: _____ DATE: _____

 DIRECTIONS: Show two ways to solve the problem.

1. Find the volume of the figure by breaking it apart into two rectangular prisms. Draw the two prisms, write their dimensions, and find the volume.

5 m

5 m   8 m

7 m   7 m

Strategy 1

Strategy 2

2. Does it matter which strategy you use to find the volume of the figure? Why or why not?

_____

_____

_____

_____

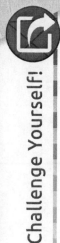

NAME: _____ **DATE:** _____

 Read and solve the problem.

Maritza works at a pet store. She is in charge of designing the hamster display. The display needs to be made of two connected rectangular prisms. It must be a total of 500 cubic feet. Sketch a design for the display. Label the dimensions, and prove that it has a total volume of 500 cubic feet.

1. Show your design and label the dimensions.

2. Prove that the total volume is 500 cubic feet.

3. Can you think of a different way to design the display? Explain your thinking.

_____

_____

_____

NAME: _____ DATE: _____

 DIRECTIONS: Think about the problem, and answer the questions.

Marcy is making food for her dog. She uses $\frac{1}{3}$ cup of peanut butter and $\frac{4}{9}$ cup of rolled oats. How many cups of food does she make altogether?

1. Which set of equivalent fractions can be used to solve the problem? Select all that apply.

   A. $\frac{1}{9}$ and $\frac{4}{9}$

   B. $\frac{3}{9}$ and $\frac{4}{9}$

   C. $\frac{7}{9}$ and $\frac{4}{9}$

   D. $\frac{9}{27}$ and $\frac{12}{27}$

2. How do you know the fractions you chose are equivalent to the fractions in the problem?

   _____

   _____

   _____

3. Which set of equivalent fractions would you use to solve the problem? Explain your reasoning.

   _____

   _____

   _____

NAME: _____ **DATE:** _____

DIRECTIONS: Read and solve each problem.

Solve It!

Problem 1: Marcy is making food for her dog. She uses $\frac{1}{3}$ cup of peanut butter and $\frac{4}{9}$ cup of rolled oats. How many cups of food does she make altogether?

 What Do You Know?

 What Is Your Plan?

 Solve the Problem!

 Look Back and Explain!

Problem 2: Marcy makes a different dog food recipe. She uses $\frac{1}{4}$ cup of yogurt and $\frac{3}{8}$ cup of strawberries. How many cups of food does she make altogether?

 What Do You Know?

 What Is Your Plan?

 Solve the Problem!

 Look Back and Explain!

NAME: _____ DATE: _____

DIRECTIONS: Look at the example. Then, solve the problem.

Example: Show each fraction on a number line. Then, add the fractions by making equivalent fractions on the third number line.

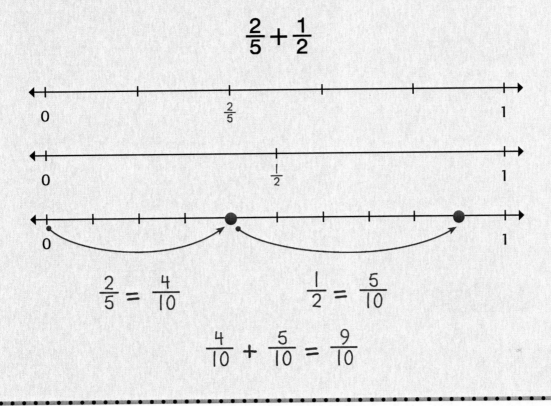

$$\frac{2}{5} + \frac{1}{2}$$

$$\frac{2}{5} = \frac{4}{10} \qquad \frac{1}{2} = \frac{5}{10}$$

$$\frac{4}{10} + \frac{5}{10} = \frac{9}{10}$$

Show each fraction on a number line. Then, add the fractions by making equivalent fractions on the third number line.

$$\frac{2}{3} + \frac{1}{4}$$

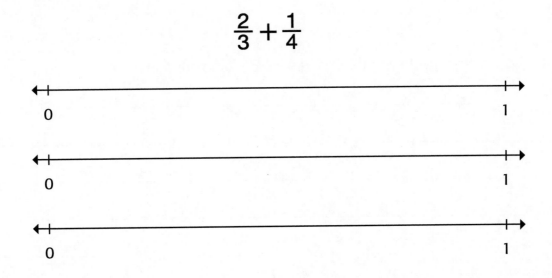

Solve It Two Ways!

NAME: _____ **DATE:** _____

DIRECTIONS: Show two ways to solve the problem.

1. The sum of two mixed numbers with unlike denominators is $3\frac{9}{12}$. Write two addition problems that have a sum of $3\frac{9}{12}$. Use words, numbers, or pictures to show your work.

Strategy 1 ·

Strategy 2 ·

2. Which strategy do you think is easier? Explain your reasoning.

_____

_____

_____

_____

_____

NAME: _____ DATE: _____

DIRECTIONS: Read and solve the problem.

Kyoko is a hairdresser. She uses fractions to mix hair color for her clients. For one client, she uses $1\frac{1}{5}$ cup medium brown, $\frac{1}{3}$ cup caramel blonde, and $\frac{1}{6}$ cup auburn red. How many cups of hair color does Kyoko use in total?

1. Draw a model to show the problem.

2. Write an equation to solve the problem.

Think About It!

NAME: _____ **DATE:** _____

DIRECTIONS: Think about the problem, and answer the questions.

Brady has $\frac{4}{5}$ of a chocolate bar. He gives $\frac{3}{10}$ of the chocolate bar to his friend. How much of the chocolate bar is left?

1. Which set of equivalent fractions can be used to solve the problem? Select all that apply.

   A. $\frac{8}{10}$ and $\frac{3}{10}$

   B. $\frac{4}{5}$ and $\frac{3}{5}$

   C. $\frac{9}{10}$ and $\frac{3}{10}$

   D. $\frac{40}{50}$ and $\frac{15}{50}$

2. How do you know the fractions you chose are equivalent to the fractions in the problem?

   _____

   _____

   _____

3. Which set of equivalent fractions would you use to solve the problem? Explain your reasoning.

   _____

   _____

   _____

   _____

NAME: _____ DATE: _____

 **DIRECTIONS:** Read and solve each problem.

Solve It!

Problem 1: Brady has $\frac{4}{5}$ of a chocolate bar. He gives $\frac{3}{10}$ of the chocolate bar to his friend. How much of the chocolate bar is left?

 What Do You Know?

 What Is Your Plan?

 Solve the Problem!

 Look Back and Explain!

Problem 2: Ravi has $\frac{3}{4}$ of a sandwich. He eats $\frac{5}{12}$ of it. How much of the sandwich is left?

 What Do You Know?

 What Is Your Plan?

 Solve the Problem!

 Look Back and Explain!

Visualize It!

NAME: _____ **DATE:** _____

DIRECTIONS: Look at the example. Then, solve the problem.

Example: Subtract the fractions by making equivalent fractions.

$$2\frac{3}{4} - 1\frac{2}{3} = \boxed{}$$

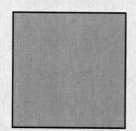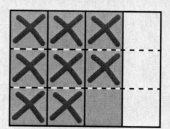

$$2\frac{9}{12} - 1\frac{8}{12} = 1\frac{1}{12}$$

1. Subtract the fractions by making equivalent fractions.

$$1\frac{5}{6} - \frac{1}{2} = \boxed{}$$

2. How can you choose a common denominator for the fractions?

_____

_____

_____

NAME: _____ **DATE:** _____

DIRECTIONS: Show two ways to solve the problem.

1. Holly makes a goal to run 1 mile every day. She runs $\frac{3}{8}$ of a mile to her grandmother's house and then $\frac{1}{4}$ of a mile to the store. What fraction of a mile does Holly have left to reach her goal?

> Strategy 1

· ·

> Strategy 2

· ·

2. Which strategy do you think is easier? Explain your reasoning.

_____

_____

_____

_____

_____

Challenge Yourself!

NAME: _____ **DATE:** _____

DIRECTIONS: Read and solve the problem.

Zooland has two sloths. Suzy Sloth sleeps $\frac{2}{3}$ of the day.
Sammi Sloth sleeps $\frac{5}{6}$ of the day. Which sloth sleeps longer?
How much longer?

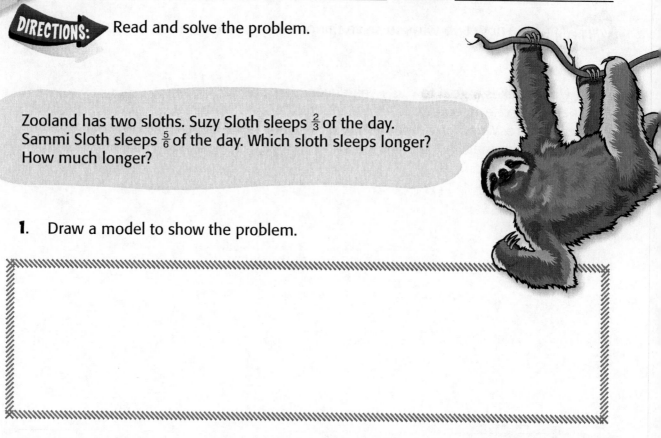

1. Draw a model to show the problem.

2. Compare the fractions using >, <, or = . Write an equation to solve the problem.

3. How many hours longer does this sloth sleep?

NAME: _____ **DATE:** _____

DIRECTIONS: Think about the problem, and answer the questions.

Jeff and Annie want to roast marshmallows. Jeff has $\frac{1}{8}$ of a bag of marshmallows. Annie has $\frac{1}{3}$ of a bag of marshmallows. If they combine their marshmallows, what fraction of a bag do they have altogether?

Think About It!

1. What information is given?

   _____

   _____

2. Do you think the solution will be greater than 1 or less than 1? Why do you think so?

   _____

   _____

   _____

3. What common denominator would you choose to solve the problem? Explain your reasoning.

   _____

   _____

   _____

Solve It!

NAME: _____ **DATE:** _____

 DIRECTIONS: Read and solve each problem.

Problem 1: Jeff and Annie want to roast marshmallows. Jeff has $\frac{1}{8}$ of a bag of marshmallows. Annie has $\frac{1}{3}$ of a bag of marshmallows. If they combine their marshmallows, what fraction of a bag do they have altogether?

 What Do You Know?

 What Is Your Plan?

 Solve the Problem!

 Look Back and Explain!

Problem 2: D'Sean and Jada have $3\frac{3}{4}$ cups of trail mix. They eat $1\frac{1}{2}$ cups of trail mix. How many cups of trail mix is left?

 What Do You Know?

 What Is Your Plan?

 Solve the Problem!

 Look Back and Explain!

NAME: _____   **DATE:** _____

DIRECTIONS: Look at the example. Then, solve the problem.

Example: Gina is making cookies. The recipe calls for $1\frac{1}{2}$ cups of sugar and $2\frac{1}{8}$ cups of flour. Her bowl holds 4 cups. Will the ingredients fit in the bowl? How many cups of ingredients does she have altogether?

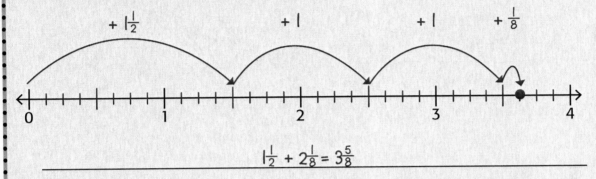

$$1\frac{1}{2} + 2\frac{1}{8} = 3\frac{5}{8}$$

Yes, the ingredients will fit in the bowl because $3\frac{5}{8}$ is less than 4.

Gina is also making a salad. The recipe calls for $1\frac{5}{6}$ cups of sliced tomatoes and $\frac{2}{3}$ cup of sliced cucumber. Her mixing bowl holds 3 cups. Will the ingredients fit in the bowl? How many cups of ingredients does she have altogether?

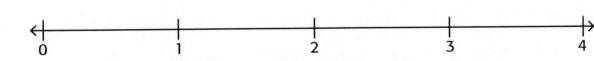

_____

_____

Solve It Two Ways!

NAME: _____ **DATE:** _____

DIRECTIONS: Show two ways to solve the problem.

1. Otis wants to bake an apple crisp. The recipe requires 1 cup of flour. Otis has $\frac{1}{3}$ cup of flour in one bag and $\frac{3}{5}$ cup of flour in another bag. Does he have enough flour to bake the apple crisp?

Strategy 1

Strategy 2

2. Which strategy do you like better? Explain your reasoning.

_____

_____

_____

_____

_____

NAME: _____ DATE: _____

DIRECTIONS: Read and solve the problem.

Crystal drinks $1\frac{1}{5}$ liters of water a day. Her little brother drinks $\frac{3}{10}$ liter of water a day. How many more liters of water does Crystal drink than her brother? How many liters of water do they drink altogether?

1. Use words, numbers, or pictures to show how many more liters Crystal drinks than her brother.

2. Use equations to show how many liters they drink altogether.

Think About It!

NAME: _____ DATE: _____

DIRECTIONS: Think about the problem, and answer the questions.

Four brownies are shared equally among 3 friends. What fraction of the brownies does each friend get?

1. Will each friend get more than 1 or less than 1 brownie? How do you know?

_____

_____

_____

_____

_____

2. What expressions can you write to solve this problem?

_____

_____

_____

_____

_____

_____

NAME: _____ DATE: _____

 DIRECTIONS: Read and solve each problem.

Problem 1: Four brownies are shared equally among 3 friends. What fraction of the brownies does each friend get?

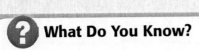 **What Do You Know?**

 **What Is Your Plan?**

Solve the Problem!

Look Back and Explain!

Problem 2: The 12 members of the math club are sharing 4 boxes of crackers. What fraction of a box does each member get?

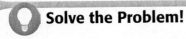 **What Do You Know?**

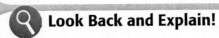 **What Is Your Plan?**

 Solve the Problem!

 Look Back and Explain!

Visualize It!

NAME: _____ **DATE:** _____

 **DIRECTIONS:** Look at the example. Then, solve the problem.

Example: Four friends share 5 small pizzas. What fraction of the pizza does each friend get?

 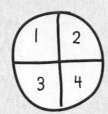 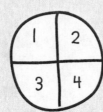 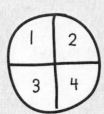 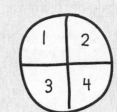

$$\frac{1}{4} + \frac{1}{4} + \frac{1}{4} + \frac{1}{4} + \frac{1}{4} = \frac{5}{4}$$

$$5 \div 4 = \frac{5}{4} = 1\frac{1}{4}$$

Six friends share 8 small quesadillas. What fraction of the quesadillas does each friend get?

_____

_____

NAME: _____ **DATE:** _____

DIRECTIONS: Show two ways to solve the problem.

1. A restaurant has 3 pans of lasagna. The lasagna will be shared among 8 customers. What fraction of the lasagna will each customer receive?

Strategy 1

Draw a fraction model.

Strategy 2

Write a division expression and fraction.

2. Which strategy do you think is better? Explain your reasoning.

_____

_____

_____

_____

_____

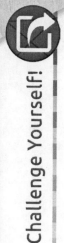

NAME: _____ **DATE:** _____

DIRECTIONS: Read and solve the problem.

At Outdoor Adventure Campground, campers can sit at tables with 8 chairs or 10 chairs. Six pizzas are served at tables with 8 chairs. Eight pizzas are served at the tables with 10 chairs. Pizzas are divided equally at each table. Which table should campers sit at if they want the most pizza possible?

1. Draw a model to show how much pizza each person will get at the tables with 8 chairs.

2. Draw a model to show how much pizza each person will get at the tables with 10 chairs.

3. At which table will campers get the most pizza? Explain your reasoning.

_____

_____

NAME: _____ **DATE:** _____

DIRECTIONS: Think about the problem, and answer the questions.

Toby has a picture frame on his bedroom wall. It is a rectangle measuring 3 feet tall and $\frac{3}{4}$ foot wide. What is the area of the picture frame?

Think About It!

1. Will the area of the poster be greater than 3 square feet or less than 3 square feet? How do you know?

_____

_____

_____

2. What repeated addition expression can be used to solve the problem?

_____

_____

_____

3. What multiplication expression can be used to solve the problem?

_____

_____

_____

_____

Solve It!

NAME: _____ **DATE:** _____

DIRECTIONS: Read and solve each problem.

Problem 1: Toby has a picture frame on his bedroom wall. It is a rectangle measuring 3 feet tall and $\frac{3}{4}$ foot wide. What is the area of the picture frame?

 What Do You Know?

 What Is Your Plan?

 Solve the Problem!

 Look Back and Explain!

Problem 2: Sabrina has a picture frame on her bedroom wall. It is a rectangle measuring 2 feet tall and $\frac{2}{3}$ foot wide. What is the area of the picture frame?

 What Do You Know?

 What Is Your Plan?

 Solve the Problem!

 Look Back and Explain!

NAME: _____ **DATE:** _____

DIRECTIONS: Look at the example. Then, solve the problem.

Example:

$$5 \times \frac{1}{3} = \boxed{}$$

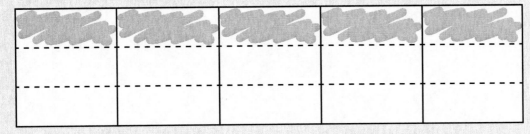

$$\frac{1}{3} + \frac{1}{3} + \frac{1}{3} + \frac{1}{3} + \frac{1}{3} = \frac{5}{3} = 1\frac{2}{3}$$

$$5 \times \frac{1}{3} = \frac{5}{3} = 1\frac{2}{3}$$

$$8 \times \frac{5}{6} = \boxed{}$$

Solve It Two Ways!

NAME: _____ **DATE:** _____

DIRECTIONS: Show two ways to solve the problem.

1. Kimi runs $\frac{3}{4}$ of a mile every day. How many miles does she run in one week?

Strategy 1 ·

Strategy 2 ·

2. Which strategy do you like better? Explain your reasoning.

_____

_____

_____

_____

_____

NAME: _____ **DATE:** _____

DIRECTIONS: Read and solve the problem.

An electric pencil sharpener at South Middle School was used 60 times on Friday. Sixth graders used it $\frac{2}{5}$ of the time. Seventh graders used it $\frac{1}{3}$ of the time. The fifth graders used it the rest of the time. How many times did the fifth graders use the pencil sharpener?

Challenge Yourself!

1. Use equations to show the number of times the sixth graders used the pencil sharpener.

2. Use equations to show the number of times the seventh graders used the pencil sharpener.

3. Show how you found the number of times the fifth graders used the pencil sharpener. Explain your thinking.

_____

_____

Think About It!

NAME: _____ **DATE:** _____

DIRECTIONS: Think about the problem, and answer the questions.

Jermaine works at Foot Works shoe store. He knows $\frac{3}{5}$ of the shoes in the store are athletic shoes. He notices that $\frac{1}{4}$ of the athletic shoes are blue. What fraction of all the shoes are blue athletic shoes?

1. What information is given?

_____

_____

_____

2. How can you solve the problem?

_____

_____

_____

3. Will the solution be less than $\frac{3}{5}$ or greater than $\frac{3}{5}$? How do you know?

_____

_____

_____

_____

#51617—180 Days of Problem Solving
© Shell Education

NAME: _____ **DATE:** _____

 DIRECTIONS: Read and solve each problem.

Problem 1: Jermaine works at Foot Works shoe store. He knows $\frac{3}{5}$ of the shoes in the store are athletic shoes. He notices that $\frac{1}{4}$ of the athletic shoes are blue. What fraction of all the shoes are blue athletic shoes?

 What Do You Know?

 What Is Your Plan?

 Solve the Problem!

 Look Back and Explain!

Problem 2: Jan works at I ♥ Fashion clothing store. She knows $\frac{5}{8}$ of the pants in the store are jeans. She notices that $\frac{2}{3}$ of the jeans are blue. What fraction of all the pants are blue jeans?

What Do You Know?

What Is Your Plan?

 Solve the Problem!

 Look Back and Explain!

Visualize It!

NAME: _____ DATE: _____

DIRECTIONS: Look at the example. Then, solve the problem.

Example:

$$\frac{2}{3} \times \frac{3}{5} = \boxed{\frac{6}{15}}$$

$\frac{3}{5}$

$\frac{2}{3}$

$$\frac{3}{4} \times \frac{1}{2} = \boxed{}$$

NAME: _____ **DATE:** _____

DIRECTIONS: Show two ways to solve the problem.

1. An ice cream shop has $\frac{5}{6}$ of a tub of chocolate ice cream. Alicia buys $\frac{1}{2}$ of the chocolate ice cream for a party. What fraction of the ice cream does she buy?

· · · · Strategy 1 ·

· · · · Strategy 2 ·

2. Which strategy do you like better? Explain your reasoning.

_____

_____

_____

_____

_____

NAME: _____ **DATE:** _____

DIRECTIONS: Read and solve the problem.

Reanna is a graphic artist who paints and decorates store windows. A coffee shop wants her to decorate a rectangular window. It measures $\frac{9}{10}$ meter by $\frac{4}{5}$ meter. Reanna charges $100 per square meter. How much will the coffee shop pay Reanna?

1. Draw a model to show how many square meters make up the window.

2. Use equations to show how much Reanna will get paid. Explain your thinking.

_____

_____

_____

NAME: _____ **DATE:** _____

DIRECTIONS: Think about the problem, and answer the questions.

The students at Fairmont School are decorating bulletin boards. The fifth-grade bulletin board is 3 meters long and $\frac{7}{10}$ meter tall. The sixth-grade bulletin board is 3 meters long and $\frac{12}{10}$ meters tall. Which grade-level's bulletin board has a greater area?

Think About It!

1. Is the area of the fifth-grade bulletin board greater than or less than 3 square meters? How do you know?

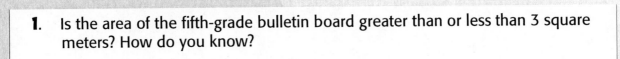

_____

_____

_____

_____

_____

2. Is the area of the sixth-grade bulletin board greater than or less than 3 square meters? How do you know?

_____

_____

_____

_____

_____

NAME: _____ DATE: _____

Solve It!

DIRECTIONS: Read and solve each problem.

Problem 1: The students at Fairmont School are decorating bulletin boards. The fifth-grade bulletin board is 3 meters long and $\frac{7}{10}$ meter tall. The sixth-grade bulletin board is 3 meters long and $\frac{12}{10}$ meter tall. Which grade-level's bulletin board has a greater area?

 What Do You Know?

 What Is Your Plan?

 Solve the Problem!

 Look Back and Explain!

Problem 2: One-third of the seventh-grade bulletin board is red. Half of the red section is used to display science projects. Half of the eighth-grade bulletin board is red. One-third of the red section is used to display science projects. Which grade level has a larger display area for science projects?

 What Do You Know?

 What Is Your Plan?

 Solve the Problem!

 Look Back and Explain!

NAME: _____ DATE: _____

 DIRECTIONS: Look at the example. Then, solve the problem.

Example: Michelle, Ashley, and Jessica are competitive figure skaters. Michelle scores a 7 on her performance. Ashley's score is $\frac{5}{6}$ of Michelle's score. Jessica's score is $\frac{3}{4}$ of Michelle's score. Did Ashley or Jessica receive a higher score?

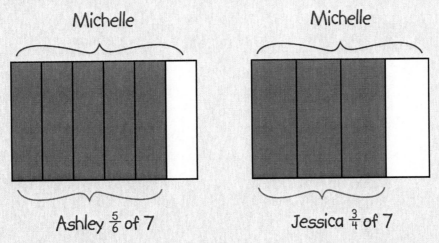

Ashley receives a higher score because $\frac{5}{6}$ is greater than $\frac{3}{4}$.

Greg, Danny, and Kenny are also competitive figure skaters. Greg scores an 8 on his performance. Danny's score is $\frac{3}{5}$ of Greg's score. Kenny's score is $\frac{7}{8}$ of Greg's score. Did Danny or Kenny receive a higher score?

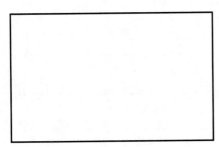   

_____

_____

Solve It Two Ways!

NAME: _____ **DATE:** _____

DIRECTIONS: Show two ways to solve the problem.

1. Write a multiplication problem that will give a product less than $3\frac{1}{3}$. Then, write a different multiplication problem that will give a product greater than $3\frac{1}{3}$. Use $3\frac{1}{3}$ as one of the factors for each problem. Show your work to prove the problems are correct.

· · · · Strategy 1 ·

· · · · Strategy 2 ·

2. What strategies did you use to choose the other factor for each problem?

_____

_____

_____

_____

NAME: _____ **DATE:** _____

DIRECTIONS: Read and solve the problem.

Myla is a florist at Petal Creations flower shop. She makes bouquets based on the number of roses purchased. A customer receives $\frac{4}{3}$ as many daisies as roses and $\frac{2}{3}$ as many carnations as roses. Kevin buys 6 roses.

1. Show how to determine what flower Kevin receives the most of in his bouquet.

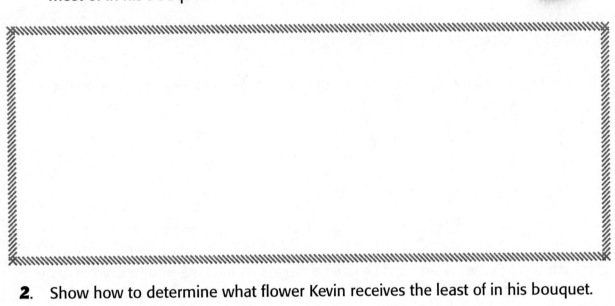

2. Show how to determine what flower Kevin receives the least of in his bouquet.

Think About It!

NAME: _____   DATE: _____

DIRECTIONS: Think about the problem, and answer the questions.

Sydney has $5\frac{1}{2}$ boxes of cookies. Three-fifths of them are chocolate chip. What fraction of the boxes of cookies are chocolate chip?

1. Sydney writes multiplication equations to find the solution. Are her calculations correct so far? Explain your thinking.

$$\frac{3}{5} \times 5 = \frac{15}{5} \qquad \frac{3}{5} \times \frac{1}{2} = \frac{3}{10}$$

_____

_____

2. Which of Sydney's products can be expressed as a whole number? What is the whole number?

_____

_____

3. What step does Sydney need to do next?

_____

_____

NAME: _____ DATE: _____

 DIRECTIONS: Read and solve each problem.

Solve It!

Problem 1: Sydney has $5\frac{1}{2}$ boxes of cookies. Three-fifths of them are chocolate chip. What fraction of the boxes of cookies are chocolate chip?

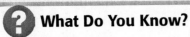 **What Do You Know?**

 What Is Your Plan?

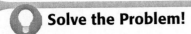 **Solve the Problem!**

 Look Back and Explain!

Problem 2: Sydney also has $1\frac{7}{10}$ quarts of milk. She drinks $\frac{3}{8}$ of it. How much milk does Sydney drink?

 What Do You Know?

 What Is Your Plan?

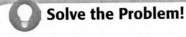 **Solve the Problem!**

 Look Back and Explain!

Visualize It!

NAME: _____ **DATE:** _____

DIRECTIONS: Look at the example. Then, solve the problem.

Example:

$$1\frac{1}{4} \times 2\frac{2}{3} = \boxed{}$$

×	2	$\frac{2}{3}$
1	2	$\frac{2}{3}$
$\frac{1}{4}$	$\frac{2}{4}$	$\frac{2}{12}$

$$2 + \frac{2}{3} + \frac{2}{4} + \frac{2}{12}$$

$$2 + \frac{8}{12} + \frac{6}{12} + \frac{2}{12}$$

$$2\frac{16}{12} = 3\frac{4}{12} = 3\frac{1}{3}$$

$$3\frac{1}{6} \times 2\frac{1}{2} = \boxed{}$$

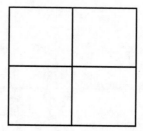

_____

_____

_____

NAME: _____ DATE: _____

DIRECTIONS: Show two ways to solve the problem.

1. The football team sells rectangular banners measuring $1\frac{3}{4}$ feet across and $\frac{3}{4}$ foot wide. What is the area of one banner?

Strategy 1

Strategy 2

2. Which strategy do you think is better? Explain your reasoning.

_____

_____

_____

_____

_____

Challenge Yourself!

NAME: _____ **DATE:** _____

DIRECTIONS: Read and solve the problem.

Greta and her friends make some trail mix. She uses $2\frac{1}{2}$ cups of raisins for her recipe. Rick triples the amount of Greta's raisins in his recipe. Charlotte uses $\frac{4}{5}$ the amount of Greta's raisins in her recipe. Ellen uses $1\frac{1}{2}$ times the amount of Greta's raisins in her recipe.

1. Show how to find the amount of raisins in Rick's recipe.

2. Show how to find the amount of raisins in Charlotte's recipe.

3. Show how to find the amount of raisins in Ellen's recipe.

4. How do you know who has the most raisins in their recipe? Explain your thinking.

_____

_____

NAME: _____ DATE: _____

DIRECTIONS: Think about the problem, and answer the questions.

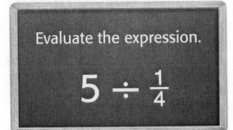

Evaluate the expression.

$$5 \div \frac{1}{4}$$

1. Which of the following story problems matches $5 \div \frac{1}{4}$? Select all that apply.

   A. Eric drives 5 miles to work. He has driven $\frac{1}{4}$ of the way. How many miles has he driven so far?

   B. Renee has 5 blocks of mozzarella cheese. Each small pizza requires $\frac{1}{4}$ block of cheese. How many pizzas can she make?

   C. Elyse has a licorice rope measuring 5 feet long. She wants to give her friends $\frac{1}{4}$ foot each. How many friends will get licorice?

   D. Mary has 5 chocolate bars. She eats $\frac{1}{4}$ of them. How many chocolate bars did she eat?

2. Does the order of the numbers matter in the equation? Explain your thinking.

   _____

   _____

   _____

   _____

Solve It!

NAME: _____ DATE: _____

DIRECTIONS: Read and solve each problem.

Problem 1: Evaluate the expression $5 \div \frac{1}{4}$.

 What Do You Know?

 What Is Your Plan?

 Solve the Problem!

 Look Back and Explain!

Problem 2: Evaluate the expression $2 \div \frac{1}{6}$.

 What Do You Know?

 What Is Your Plan?

 Solve the Problem!

 Look Back and Explain!

#51617—180 Days of Problem Solving

NAME: _____ **DATE:** _____

 DIRECTIONS: Look at the example. Then, solve the problem.

Example: Emma has 3 feet of ribbon. She is making bows that require $\frac{1}{3}$ foot of ribbon each. How many bows can she make?

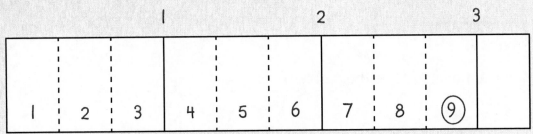

$$3 \div \frac{1}{3} = 9 \text{ bows}$$

Will needs to post track practice flyers around the school. He has 6 feet of tape. Each flyer takes $\frac{1}{2}$ foot of tape. How many flyers can he hang?

Solve It Two Ways!

NAME: _____ **DATE:** _____

DIRECTIONS: Show two ways to solve the problem.

1. A box of baby cereal contains 7 cups of cereal. Henry's baby brother eats $\frac{1}{8}$ cup for each serving. How many servings are in the box of baby cereal?

Strategy 1

Draw a model to solve the problem.

Strategy 2

Write and solve an equation.

2. Which strategy do you like better? Explain your reasoning.

_____

_____

_____

_____

_____

NAME: _____ DATE: _____

DIRECTIONS: Read and solve the problem.

Scott is making a snack using a recipe. He can only find his $\frac{1}{3}$ measuring cup.

Sweet 'n Sticky Cereal Mix

- 9 cups rice cereal
- 2 cups chocolate chips
- 1 cup creamy peanut butter

1. Draw pictures to show how many $\frac{1}{3}$ cups Scott needs for each ingredient.

2. Write equations to show how many $\frac{1}{3}$ cups Scott needs for each ingredient.

3. How many $\frac{1}{3}$ cups of ingredients does Scott use in all? Explain how you found your solution.

    _____

    _____

    _____

Think About It!

NAME: _____ DATE: _____

DIRECTIONS: Think about the problem, and answer the questions.

Marcus works at a coffee shop. There is $\frac{1}{2}$ of a bottle of caramel syrup to make flavored drinks. Marcus is able to make 10 drinks before the bottle is empty. What fraction of the entire bottle is used for each drink?

1. Complete the following statement using the information from the problem:

    The solution will be _____ (*less* or *greater*) than $\frac{1}{2}$ because Marcus

    is sharing _____ of a bottle between _____ drinks.

2. What expression can you write to solve the problem?

    _____

    _____

    _____

    _____

    _____

NAME: _____ DATE: _____

 DIRECTIONS: Read and solve each problem.

Solve It!

Problem 1: Marcus works at a coffee shop. There is $\frac{1}{2}$ of a bottle of caramel syrup to make flavored drinks. Marcus is able to make 10 drinks before the bottle is empty. What fraction of the entire bottle is used for each drink?

 What Do You Know?

 What Is Your Plan?

 Solve the Problem!

 Look Back and Explain!

Problem 2: Marcus makes many different flavored drinks at the coffee shop. There is $\frac{1}{3}$ of a bottle of chocolate syrup. Marcus is able to make 5 drinks before the bottle is empty. What fraction of the entire bottle is used for each drink?

 What Do You Know?

 What Is Your Plan?

 Solve the Problem!

 Look Back and Explain!

Visualize It!

NAME: _____ **DATE:** _____

DIRECTIONS: Look at the example. Then, solve the problem.

Example: There is $\frac{1}{4}$ of a pan of corn bread for a family of 3 to share equally. What fraction of the corn bread does each person receive?

$\frac{1}{4}$

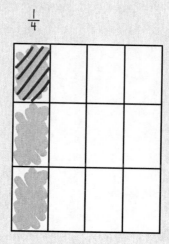

$\frac{1}{4} \div 3 = \frac{1}{12}$ of the corn bread

There is $\frac{1}{8}$ of a pan of corn bread for a family of 4 to share equally. What fraction of the corn bread does each person receive?

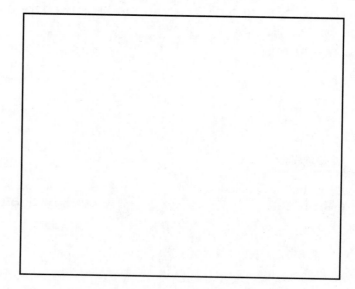

NAME: _____ **DATE:** _____

DIRECTIONS: Show two ways to solve the problem.

1. Franz has $\frac{1}{5}$ of a jumbo-size box of popcorn to share with his brother at the movie. What fraction of the popcorn will Franz and his brother each get if they share it equally?

   Strategy 1 ·

   Draw a model to solve the problem.

   Strategy 2 ·

   Write and solve an equation.

2. **Which strategy do you like better? Explain your reasoning.**

   _____

   _____

   _____

   _____

   _____

Challenge Yourself!

NAME: _____ **DATE:** _____

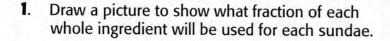

DIRECTIONS: Read and solve the problem.

Patty works at Sundaes Fun Days ice cream shop. Her boss tells her to prepare 6 identical sundaes using the ingredients shown.

- $\frac{1}{2}$ gallon vanilla ice cream
- $\frac{1}{4}$ pound chocolate chunks
- $\frac{1}{3}$ cup mini marshmallows
- $\frac{1}{5}$ jar maraschino cherries

1. Draw a picture to show what fraction of each whole ingredient will be used for each sundae.

2. Write equations to show what fraction of each whole ingredient will be used for each sundae.

3. If Patty makes 7 sundaes using the same ingredients, would each sundae have more or less of each ingredient? Explain your thinking.

_____

_____

_____

NAME: _____ DATE: _____

DIRECTIONS: Think about the problem, and answer the questions.

Lisa is making macaroni and cheese for dinner. Each serving has $\frac{1}{2}$ cup of macaroni. She has 8 cups of macaroni.

1. Complete the following statement using information you know from the problem:

   There are _____ $\frac{1}{2}$-cup servings in 1 cup of macaroni. There are _____

   total cups of macaroni. The solution must be _____

   (*less* or *greater*) than 8 cups of macaroni.

2. Write a question that can be answered from the information in the problem.

   _____

   _____

   _____

   _____

Solve It!

NAME: _____ DATE: _____

DIRECTIONS: Read and solve each problem.

Problem 1: Lisa is making macaroni and cheese for dinner. Each serving has $\frac{1}{2}$ cup of macaroni. She has 8 cups of macaroni. How many servings can she make?

 What Do You Know?

 What Is Your Plan?

 Solve the Problem!

 Look Back and Explain!

Problem 2: Lisa is also baking a cake. What fraction of the whole cake will each person receive if 4 people share $\frac{1}{2}$ of it equally?

 What Do You Know?

 What Is Your Plan?

 Solve the Problem!

 Look Back and Explain!

NAME: _____ DATE: _____

 **DIRECTIONS:** Look at the example. Then, solve the problem by completing the table.

Visualize It!

Example: Write a story problem, draw a model, and solve the equation.

Story problem	Model	Equation
Celeste has a 4-pound bag of peanuts. She leaves $\frac{1}{3}$ of a pound outside for the squirrels each week. How many weeks can she feed the squirrels with a 4-pound bag?		$4 \div \frac{1}{3} = 12$ weeks

Write a story problem, draw a model, and solve the equation.

Story problem	Model	Equation
		$\frac{1}{3} \div 4 =$

Solve It Two Ways!

NAME: _____ **DATE:** _____

DIRECTIONS: Show two ways to solve the problem.

1. Theresa works at Diva Dog Grooming. She uses 2 cups of pet shampoo each day. She uses $\frac{1}{4}$ cup for each dog's bath. How many dogs receive a bath? Look at the first strategy used to solve the problem. Then, solve the problem a different way.

Strategy 1

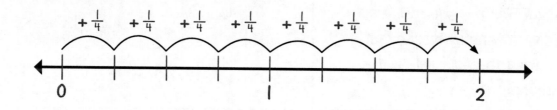

Strategy 2

2. Which strategy do you think is better? Explain your reasoning.

_____

_____

_____

_____

_____

NAME: _____ DATE: _____

DIRECTIONS: Read and solve the problem.

Valerie is making salsa using a recipe which makes 12 servings. After chopping up some fresh tomatoes, she adds the ingredients shown.

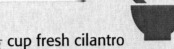

- $\frac{1}{2}$ cup fresh cilantro

- $\frac{1}{4}$ cup fresh chopped onion

- $\frac{1}{3}$ cup lime juice

- $\frac{1}{6}$ cup minced garlic

1. Draw pictures to show the fraction of the ingredients that are in each serving of salsa.

2. Write equations to show the fraction of the ingredients that are in each serving of salsa.

3. If Valerie makes 10 servings of salsa using the same ingredients, would each serving have more or less of each ingredient? Explain your thinking.

_____

_____

_____

Think About It!

NAME: _____ **DATE:** _____

DIRECTIONS: Think about the problem, and answer the questions.

James is having a birthday party. He orders a 5-foot-long submarine sandwich. Each of the 6 people at the party shares the sandwich equally. How many inches of the sandwich does each person get?

1. What information is given?

    _____

    _____

2. Does each person get more or less than 1 foot of the sandwich? How do you know?

    _____

    _____

3. How many inches are in 5 feet? Show how you know.

NAME: _____ DATE: _____

 DIRECTIONS: Read and solve each problem.

Problem 1: James is celebrating his birthday. He orders a 5-foot-long submarine sandwich. Each of the 6 people at the party shares the sandwich equally. How many inches of sandwich does each person get?

 What Do You Know?

 What Is Your Plan?

 Solve the Problem!

 Look Back and Explain!

Problem 2: Two of the 6 invited guests do not come to James's party. He decides to share the 5-foot-long sandwich equally among the 4 guests. How many inches of sandwich does each guest get?

 What Do You Know?

 What Is Your Plan?

 Solve the Problem!

 Look Back and Explain!

Visualize It!

NAME: _____ **DATE:** _____

DIRECTIONS: Look at the example. Then, solve the problem.

Example: Convert feet to inches. Write the fractions in simplest form.

Feet	Inches
0	0
$\frac{1}{4}$	3
$\frac{2}{4} = \boxed{\frac{1}{2}}$	6
$\frac{3}{4}$	9
$\frac{4}{4} = \boxed{1}$	12

$\frac{1}{4}$ of $12 = \frac{1}{4} \times \frac{12}{1} = \frac{12}{4} = 3$

$\frac{1}{2}$ of $12 = \frac{1}{2} \times \frac{12}{1} = \frac{12}{2} = 6$

$\frac{3}{4}$ of $12 = \frac{3}{4} \times \frac{12}{1} = \frac{36}{4} = 9$

Convert the number of feet to inches. Write fractions in simplest form.

Feet	Inches
0	0
$\frac{1}{6}$	
$\frac{2}{6} = \boxed{}$	
$\frac{3}{6} = \boxed{}$	
$\frac{4}{6} = \boxed{}$	

NAME: _____ **DATE:** _____

DIRECTIONS: Show two ways to solve the problem.

1. There are 10 nurses sharing one 24-hour shift at the hospital. How many hours and minutes does each nurse spend at the hospital if they each share the shift equally?

    Strategy 1

    Strategy 2

2. Which strategy do you like better? Explain your reasoning.

    _____

    _____

    _____

    _____

    _____

Challenge Yourself!

NAME: _____ **DATE:** _____

DIRECTIONS: Read and solve the problem.

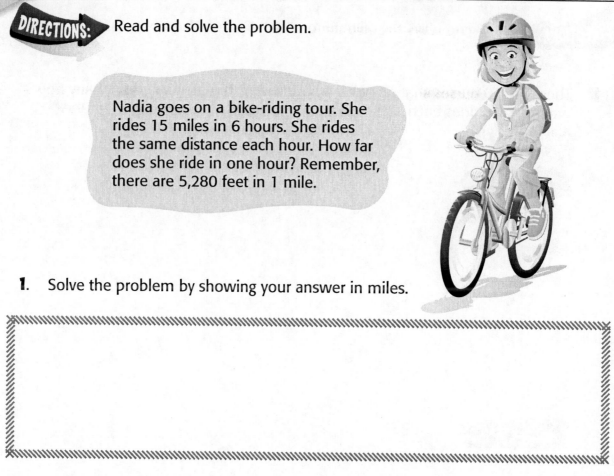

Nadia goes on a bike-riding tour. She rides 15 miles in 6 hours. She rides the same distance each hour. How far does she ride in one hour? Remember, there are 5,280 feet in 1 mile.

1. Solve the problem by showing your answer in miles.

2. Solve the problem by showing your answer in miles and feet.

3. Solve the problem by showing your answer in feet.

NAME: _____ DATE: _____

 DIRECTIONS: Think about the problem, and answer the questions.

Carol works at a cosmetics counter at a department store. She counts the perfume bottles and records the results on a line plot. How many bottles of perfume does Carol count?

Title: _____

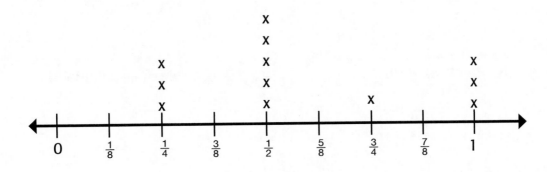

Ounces per bottle

1. What title do you think Carol should use for her line plot? Write your title at the top of the line plot.

2. How can you find the number of perfume bottles?

    _____

    _____

    _____

    _____

3. What unit is being used to measure the perfume?

    _____

NAME: _____ **DATE:** _____

 DIRECTIONS: Read and solve each problem.

Solve It!

Problem 1: Carol works at a cosmetics counter at a department store. She counts the perfume bottles and records the results on a line plot. How many bottles of perfume does Carol count?

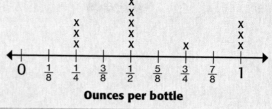

Ounces per bottle

 What Do You Know?

What Is Your Plan?

Solve the Problem!

 Look Back and Explain!

Problem 2: Carol wants to know how many ounces of perfume are in all of the bottles combined. Use the line plot in problem 1 to find the answer.

 What Do You Know?

What Is Your Plan?

 Solve the Problem!

 Look Back and Explain!

#51617—180 Days of Problem Solving

NAME: _____ DATE: _____

DIRECTIONS: Look at the example. Then, solve the problem.

Example: Brett is a chef at a restaurant. He counts the bottles of each spice and writes the number of ounces in each bottle. Make a line plot with the data shown below.

Spice	Number of bottles	Bottle size
Italian seasoning	3	$\frac{3}{4}$ ounce
dried chives	1	$\frac{1}{8}$ ounce
rosemary leaves	1	$\frac{3}{8}$ ounce
parsley flakes	2	$\frac{1}{4}$ ounce
basil leaves	3	$\frac{1}{2}$ ounce

Restaurant Spice Rack Inventory

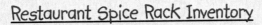

Ounces per bottle

Saul works at a bakery. He counts the spice rack bottles of each ingredient and writes the number of ounces in each bottle. Make a line plot with the data shown below.

Spice	Number of bottles	Bottle size
cinnamon	3	$4\frac{1}{8}$ ounces
ginger	2	$4\frac{1}{2}$ ounces
orange peel	1	5 ounces
vanilla extract	1	4 ounces
nutmeg	2	$4\frac{3}{4}$ ounces

Title: _____

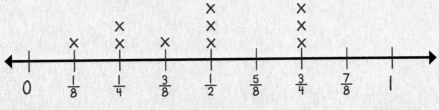

_____

NAME: _____ **DATE:** _____

DIRECTIONS: Show two ways to solve the problem.

1. Janet counts her crayons and measures them. She records the information on a line plot. If she lays all her crayons end-to-end, what is the total length of all the crayons?

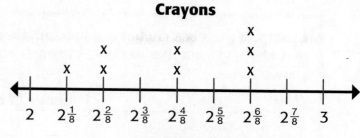

Crayons

Length (inches)

Strategy 1

Strategy 2

2. Which strategy do you think is better? Explain your reasoning.

_____

_____

_____

_____

_____

NAME: _____ DATE: _____

 DIRECTIONS: Read and solve the problem.

Dan works at Paws and Claws pet store. He records the weights, in pounds, of 10 bags of birdseed. Make a line plot to show the data.

$2\frac{1}{2}$ $2\frac{3}{4}$ $2\frac{1}{8}$ $2\frac{1}{8}$ $2\frac{5}{8}$

$2\frac{1}{8}$ $2\frac{2}{8}$ $2\frac{7}{8}$ $2\frac{1}{8}$ $2\frac{1}{2}$

1. Make a line plot. Be sure to include a title and label the axis.

Title: _____

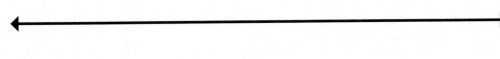

_____

2. If the birdseed is repackaged equally in all 10 bags, how much birdseed is in each bag? Show how you found your answer.

Think About It!

NAME: _____ **DATE:** _____

DIRECTIONS: Think about the problem, and answer the questions.

Sandra says that the digit 2 in 325 is 10 times greater than the digit 2 in 682. Is she correct? Why or why not?

1. What value does 2 have in 325?

_____

_____

_____

2. What value does 2 have in 682?

_____

_____

_____

3. How does understanding place value help you solve the problem?

_____

_____

_____

_____

_____

NAME: _____ **DATE:** _____

 DIRECTIONS: Read and solve each problem.

Solve It!

Problem 1: Sandra says that the digit 2 in 325 is 10 times greater than the digit 2 in 682. Is she correct? Why or why not?

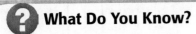 **What Do You Know?**

 What Is Your Plan?

Solve the Problem!

Look Back and Explain!

Problem 2: Jacob says that the digit 5 in 539 is $\frac{1}{10}$ the value of the digit 5 in 254. Is he correct? Why or why not?

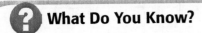 **What Do You Know?**

 What Is Your Plan?

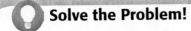 **Solve the Problem!**

 Look Back and Explain!

Visualize It!

NAME: _____ DATE: _____

DIRECTIONS: Look at the example. Then, solve the problem.

Example: Use the model to complete the statement.
Write the fraction and decimal.

The shading shows __1__ out of __10__ equal parts.

Fraction: $\frac{1}{10}$

Decimal: 0.1

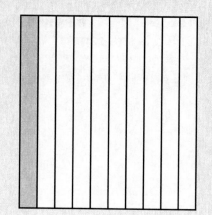

1. Use the model to complete the statement. Write the fraction and decimal.

The shading shows _____ out of _____ equal parts.

Fraction: _____

Decimal: _____

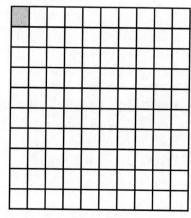

2. How many times greater is the digit 1 in 0.1 than in the decimal you wrote in problem 1? Explain your answer.

_____

_____

_____

_____

NAME: _____ **DATE:** _____

DIRECTIONS: Show two ways to solve the problem.

1. Mrs. Bradley asks her students to explain the relationship between the digits in 0.88. Billy writes two statements. Do you agree or disagree with his statements? Explain your reasoning.

Strategy 1

The 8 on the left is 100 times the value of the 8 on the right.

_____

_____

_____

_____

Strategy 2

The 8 on the right is $\frac{1}{10}$ the value of the 8 on the left.

_____

_____

_____

_____

2. How does understanding place value help you solve the problem?

_____

_____

_____

_____

_____

NAME: _____ **DATE:** _____

DIRECTIONS: Read and solve the problem.

Some jellyfish are only 0.018 meters wide. However, a lion's mane jellyfish can be 1.8 meters wide. How many times wider is the lion's mane jellyfish?

1. Draw a model to show how many times greater the digit 1 is in 1.8 than in 0.018.

2. Draw a model to show how many times greater the digit 8 is in 1.8 than in 0.018.

3. How many times wider is the lion's mane jellyfish? Show how you found your answer.

NAME: _____ DATE: _____

DIRECTIONS: Think about the problem, and answer the questions.

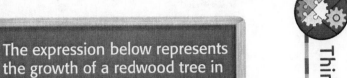

The expression below represents the growth of a redwood tree in inches. Evaluate the expression to find the height of the tree.

$$3.8 \times 10^3$$

1. Rewrite the expression by showing 10^3 two different ways.

   _____

   _____

2. Complete the statement:

   The exponent _____ indicates how many times to multiply 3.8 by

   _____ . The number becomes 10 times _____

   (*greater* or *less*) each time it is multiplied.

NAME: _____ **DATE:** _____

DIRECTIONS: Read and solve each problem.

Solve It!

Problem 1: The expression below represents the growth of a redwood tree in inches. Evaluate the expression to find the height of the tree.

$$3.8 \times 10^3$$

? What Do You Know?

🔑 What Is Your Plan?

💡 Solve the Problem!

🔍 Look Back and Explain!

Problem 2: The expression below represents the decline of a bank account, in dollars. Evaluate the expression to find how much money is in the account.

$$950 \div 10^3$$

? What Do You Know?

🔑 What Is Your Plan?

💡 Solve the Problem!

🔍 Look Back and Explain!

NAME: _____ **DATE:** _____

DIRECTIONS: Look at the examples. Then, solve the problems.

Example 1: Multiply each number by 10^1, 10^2, and 10^3.

Number	× 10^1	× 10^2	× 10^3
6.15	61.5	615	6,150
0.005	0.05	0.5	5

Example 2: Divide each number by 10^1, 10^2, and 10^3.

Number	÷ 10^1	÷ 10^2	÷ 10^3
83.2	8.32	0.832	0.0832
912.6	91.26	9.126	0.9126

1. Multiply each number by 10^1, 10^2, and 10^3.

Number	× 10^1	× 10^2	× 10^3
61.5			
0.01			

2. Divide each number by 10^1, 10^2, and 10^3.

Number	÷ 10^1	÷ 10^2	÷ 10^3
31.3			
663.4			

3. What patterns do you notice when multiplying and dividing by powers of 10?

_____

_____

_____

_____

Solve It Two Ways!

NAME: _____ **DATE:** _____

DIRECTIONS: Show two ways to solve the problem.

1. Use the given numbers to write one correct multiplication equation and one correct division equation. Show your work to prove your equations are correct.

| 47.52 | 4.752 | 100 | 10 | 475.2 | 0.4752 |

· · · · **Multiplication Equation** ·

_____ × _____ = _____

· · · · **Division Equation** ·

_____ ÷ _____ = _____

2. What strategies did you use to write the equations?

_____

_____

_____

_____

NAME: _____ DATE: _____

 DIRECTIONS: Read and solve the problem.

Evaluate each expression. Then, determine which expressions are less than 0.8, equal to 0.8, or greater than 0.8.

8×10^1	0.8×10^1	0.08×10^2	0.08×10^3
$80 \div 10^1$	$80 \div 10^3$	0.008×10^1	0.008×10^3
$0.8 \div 10^1$	0.8×10^2	$800 \div 10^2$	$800 \div 10^3$

1. Write the expressions in the correct section of the table.

Less than 0.8	Equal to 0.8	Greater than 0.8

2. What helped you determine where to write each expression?

_____

_____

_____

Challenge Yourself!

Think About It!

NAME: _____ DATE: _____

 DIRECTIONS: Think about the problem, and answer the questions.

> Matt rides his bike 0.57 kilometers to school. Write two expressions that are equivalent to 0.57.

1. How do you read 0.57 correctly? Write the decimal in word form.

_____

2. What is the equivalent fraction for 0.57?

_____

3. What digit is in the tenths place in 0.57?

_____

4. What digit is in the hundredths place in 0.57?

_____

NAME: _____ **DATE:** _____

 DIRECTIONS: Read and solve each problem.

Problem 1: Emilio rides his bike 0.57 kilometers to school. Write two expressions that are equivalent to 0.57.

 What Do You Know?

 What Is Your Plan?

 Solve the Problem!

 Look Back and Explain!

Problem 2: Marisol drives her motorcycle 3.196 kilometers to work. Write two expressions that are equivalent to 3.196.

 What Do You Know?

 What Is Your Plan?

 Solve the Problem!

 Look Back and Explain!

Visualize It!

NAME: _____ DATE: _____

DIRECTIONS: Look at the example. Then, solve the problem.

Example: Write the number in standard form, word form, fraction form, and expanded form.

Standard form	Word form	Fraction form	Expanded form
7.1	seven and one tenth	$7\frac{1}{10}$	$[(7 \times 1) + (1 \times \frac{1}{10})]$
7.18	seven and eighteen hundredths	$7\frac{18}{100}$	$(7 \times 1) + (1 \times \frac{1}{10}) + (8 \times \frac{1}{100})$
7.182	seven and one hundred eighty-two thousandths	$7\frac{182}{1,000}$	$(7 \times 1) + (1 \times \frac{1}{10}) + (8 \times \frac{1}{100}) +$ $(2 \times \frac{1}{1,000})$

Write the number in standard form, word form, fraction form, and expanded form.

Standard form	Word form	Fraction form	Expanded form
			$(2 \times 1) + (6 \times \frac{1}{10})$
	three and sixty-four hundredths		
2.086			

NAME: _____ DATE: _____

 DIRECTIONS: Show two ways to graph the decimal on a number line.

1. Jonathan wants to graph the fraction $\frac{1}{10}$ on two number lines. He notices that the number lines are labeled with decimals. Write the missing decimals on each number line. Then, make a point on each number line to show $\frac{1}{10}$.

Number Line 1

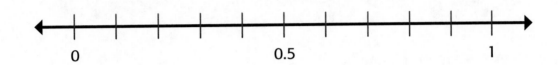

Number Line 2

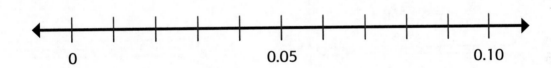

2. How are the number lines alike? How are they different?

_____

_____

_____

_____

_____

Challenge Yourself!

NAME: _____ **DATE:** _____

DIRECTIONS: Read and solve the problem.

The weight, in grams, of each gemstone is written different ways. Write the standard form for the weight of each gemstone.

Write each expression in standard form.

Sapphire

$\frac{326}{1,000}$

Garnet

$\frac{300}{1,000} + \frac{40}{1,000} + \frac{6}{1,000}$

Amethyst

$\frac{2}{10} + \frac{3}{100} + \frac{8}{1,000}$

Emerald

$(1 \times \frac{1}{10}) + (8 \times \frac{1}{100})$

Topaz

$0.600 + 0.090 + 0.002$

Diamond

thirty-two thousandths

Sapphire

_____

Garnet

_____

Amethyst

_____

Emerald

_____

Topaz

_____

Diamond

_____

NAME: _____ DATE: _____

 DIRECTIONS: Think about the problem, and answer the questions.

Madison is downloading two new game apps. Math Explorer uses 1.508 MB of storage space, and Word Catcher uses 1.57 MB of storage space. Which app uses more storage space?

1. How many ones are in 1.508? _____

How many ones are in 1.57? _____

2. How many tenths are in 1.508? _____

How many tenths are in 1.57? _____

3. How many hundredths are in 1.508? _____

How many hundredths are in 1.57? _____

4. Write 1.508 and 1.57 as fractions with denominators of 1,000.

_____

Solve It!

NAME: _____ **DATE:** _____

DIRECTIONS: Read and solve each problem.

Problem 1: Madison is downloading two new game apps. Math Explorer uses 1.508 MB of storage space, and Word Catcher uses 1.57 MB of storage space. Which amount of storage space is more?

 What Do You Know?

 What Is Your Plan?

 Solve the Problem!

 Look Back and Explain!

Problem 2: Madison wants to update two calendar apps. One uses 0.09 MB of storage space, and the other uses 0.009 MB of storage space. Which amount of storage space is less?

 What Do You Know?

 What Is Your Plan?

 Solve the Problem!

 Look Back and Explain!

NAME: _____   DATE: _____

Visualize It!

DIRECTIONS: Look at the example. Then, solve the problem.

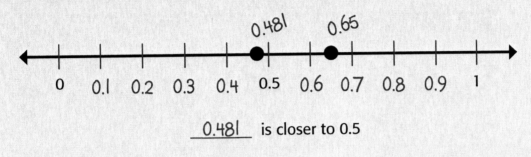

Example: Is 0.65 or 0.481 closer to 0.5 on the number line? Label each tick mark on the number line. Then, plot each decimal on the number line.

_0.481_ is closer to 0.5

1. Is 0.752 or 0.91 closer to 1 on the number line? Label each tick mark on the number line. Then, plot each decimal on the number line.

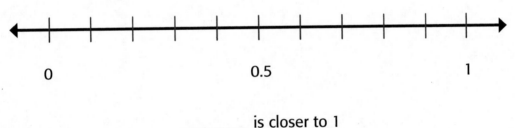

_____ is closer to 1

2. Is 0.01 or 0.1 closer to 0 on the number line? Label each tick mark on the number line. Then, plot each decimal on the number line.

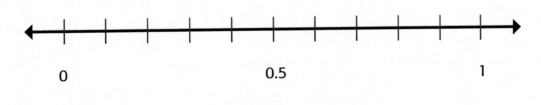

_____ is closer to 0

NAME: _____ **DATE:** _____

DIRECTIONS: Show two ways to solve the problem.

Solve It Two Ways!

1. Name three numbers that are greater than 3.14, but less than 3.15. Show your answers using words, numbers, or pictures.

> Strategy 1

> Strategy 2

2. Which strategy do you think is better? Explain your reasoning.

_____

_____

_____

_____

_____

NAME: _____ DATE: _____

DIRECTIONS: Read and solve the problem.

Challenge Yourself!

The girls basketball team at Wilson High School measures their vertical jumps. The coach records each player's jump in inches. The goal is for all of the players to jump at least 19.75 inches. Which vertical jumps are less than 19.75? Which vertical jumps are greater than 19.75?

Player name	Vertical jump
Cathy	19.7
Lynn	19.82
Darlene	19.073
Brenda	19.9
Dominique	19.743
Emily	19.751
Jackie	20.1
Angela	19.73

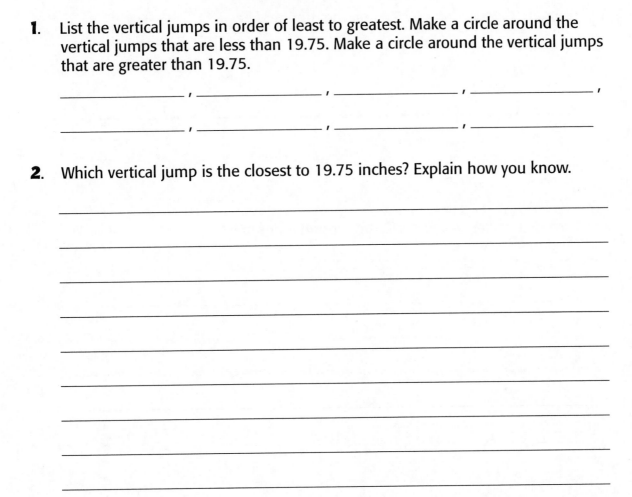

1. List the vertical jumps in order of least to greatest. Make a circle around the vertical jumps that are less than 19.75. Make a circle around the vertical jumps that are greater than 19.75.

   _____ , _____ , _____ , _____ ,

   _____ , _____ , _____ , _____

2. Which vertical jump is the closest to 19.75 inches? Explain how you know.

   _____

   _____

   _____

   _____

   _____

   _____

   _____

   _____

   _____

Think About It!

NAME: _____   DATE: _____

DIRECTIONS: Think about the problem, and answer the questions.

Rodney records the amount of gasoline he puts into his car. He puts in 7.227 gallons of gasoline on Monday. If he rounds the number of gallons to the nearest tenth, what decimal should he record?

1. Estimate the location of 7.227 on the number line.

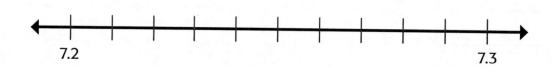

7.2   7.3

2. How does a number line help you round a number?

_____

_____

_____

_____

_____

NAME: _____ DATE: _____

 DIRECTIONS: Read and solve each problem.

Problem 1: Rodney records the amount of gasoline he puts into his car. He puts in 7.227 gallons of gasoline on Monday. If he rounds the number of gallons to the nearest tenth, what decimal should he record?

 What Do You Know?

 What Is Your Plan?

 Solve the Problem!

 Look Back and Explain!

Problem 2: On Saturday, Rodney puts 8.695 gallons of gasoline into his car. If he rounds the number of gallons to the nearest tenth, what decimal should he record?

 What Do You Know?

 What Is Your Plan?

 Solve the Problem!

 Look Back and Explain!

Visualize It!

NAME: _____ **DATE:** _____

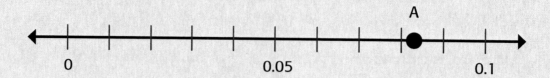

DIRECTIONS: Look at the example. Then, solve the problem.

Example: Use the number line to complete the statements.

A

← | | | | | | | | ●A | | →
0   0.05   0.1

Point A is between __0.08__ and __0.09__ .

Rounded to the nearest hundredth, Point A is __0.08__ .

Rounded to the nearest tenth, Point A is __0.1__ .

Use the number line to complete the statements.

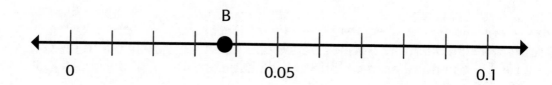

B

← | | | | ●B | | | | | | →
0   0.05   0.1

Point B is between _____ and _____ .

Rounded to the nearest hundredth, Point B is _____ .

Rounded to the nearest tenth, Point B is _____ .

NAME: _____ **DATE:** _____

DIRECTIONS: Show two ways to solve the problem.

1. Name three numbers that, when rounded to the nearest tenth, give a result of 11.2. Show your answers using words, numbers, or pictures.

Strategy 1 ·

Strategy 2 ·

2. Which strategy do you think is easier? Explain your reasoning.

_____

_____

_____

_____

_____

NAME: _____ **DATE:** _____

Read and solve the problem.

Salma measures the length of five bean plants for her science experiment. She measures each plant to the nearest thousandth of a centimeter. Then, she rounds each length to the nearest tenth and hundredth of a centimeter.

Starting decimal	Decimal rounded to the nearest tenth	Decimal rounded to the nearest hundredth
	0.4	0.43
	3.6	3.58
	9.9	9.91
	6.2	6.22
	0.1	0.09

1. Complete the table by writing one possible decimal that will round to the given decimals.

2. Can there be more than one possible starting decimal? Explain your thinking.

_____

_____

_____

_____

NAME: _____ DATE: _____

 DIRECTIONS: Think about the problem, and answer the questions.

Laurie and Kenny each buy a frozen yogurt. Laurie's yogurt weighs 12.26 ounces, and Kenny's weighs 12.43 ounces. What is the total weight of both yogurts?

Think About It!

1. Will the sum be greater than or less than 24 ounces? How do you know?

_____

_____

_____

_____

2. Will the sum be greater than or less than 25 ounces? How do you know?

_____

_____

_____

_____

#51617—180 Days of Problem Solving

Solve It!

NAME: _____ **DATE:** _____

 DIRECTIONS: Read and solve each problem.

Problem 1: Laurie and Kenny each buy a frozen yogurt. Laurie's yogurt weighs 12.26 ounces, and Kenny's weighs 12.43 ounces. What is the total weight of both yogurts?

 What Do You Know?

 What Is Your Plan?

 Solve the Problem!

 Look Back and Explain!

Problem 2: Zara buys 8 ounces of frozen yogurt. She asks for her toppings in a separate container. Her toppings include 4.4 ounces of raspberries and 1.36 ounces of crumbled chocolate cookies. What is the combined weight of her yogurt and the toppings?

 What Do You Know?

 What Is Your Plan?

 Solve the Problem!

 Look Back and Explain!

#51617—180 Days of Problem Solving

NAME: _____ **DATE:** _____

DIRECTIONS: Look at the example. Then, solve the problem.

Example: Use the number line to add the decimals in any order.

1.75 + 0.20 + 0.8

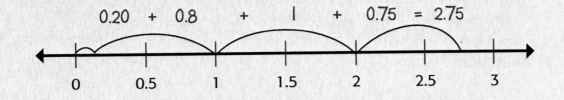

0.20 + 0.8 + 1 + 0.75 = 2.75

0 0.5 1 1.5 2 2.5 3

1.75 + 0.20 + 0.8 = ___2.75___

Use the number line to add the decimals in any order.

0.35 + 1.23 + 0.65

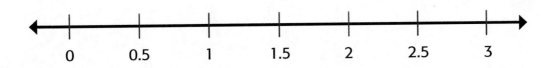

0 0.5 1 1.5 2 2.5 3

0.35 + 1.23 + 0.65 = _____

Solve It Two Ways!

NAME: _____ **DATE:** _____

DIRECTIONS: Show two ways to solve the problem.

1. David has $10.00 to spend on snacks at the baseball game. He wants to buy as many items as possible without spending more than $10.00. What items can David buy? How much does he spend? Use estimation to help you solve the problem.

Menu

Water $2.75

Hot dog $3.00

Hamburger $4.75

Popcorn $1.75

Licorice $0.75

Strategy 1

Strategy 2

2. Which strategy do you prefer? Explain your reasoning.

_____

_____

_____

_____

_____

NAME: _____   **DATE:** _____

DIRECTIONS: Read and solve the problem.

Stuart's grandmother buys him a bonus card for the arcade. It is loaded with points he can use to purchase games, prizes, and snacks. He spends 80.65 points on games, 53.62 points on snacks, 10.95 points on prizes, 1.68 points on a souvenir sticker, and 2.4 points on a souvenir pin. He only has 0.7 points left on his bonus card at the end of the day. How many points were originally on Stuart's card?

1. Show how you found the number of points Stuart used for games, prizes, and snacks.

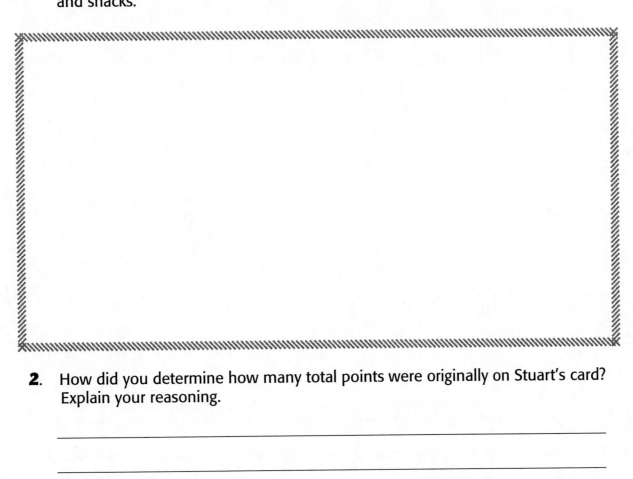

2. How did you determine how many total points were originally on Stuart's card? Explain your reasoning.

_____

_____

_____

Think About It!

NAME: _____ DATE: _____

DIRECTIONS: Think about the problem, and answer the questions.

> Quinn's Siberian husky weighs 52.75 pounds. Her Chihuahua weighs 6.5 pounds. How many more pounds does her Siberian husky weigh than her Chihuahua?

1. Quinn solves the problem as shown. Is her answer reasonable? Why or why not?

$$\begin{array}{r} 52.75 \\ -\ 6.5 \\ \hline 52.10 \end{array}$$

_____

_____

_____

2. What error did Quinn make?

_____

_____

_____

_____

NAME: _____ DATE: _____

 DIRECTIONS: Read and solve each problem.

Problem 1: Quinn's Siberian husky weighs 52.75 pounds. Her Chihuahua weighs 6.5 pounds. How many more pounds does her Siberian husky weigh than her Chihuahua?

 What Do You Know?

 What Is Your Plan?

 Solve the Problem!

 Look Back and Explain!

Problem 2: Quinn's gerbil weighs 1.4 ounces. Her hamster weighs 0.88 ounces. How many more ounces does her gerbil weigh than her hamster?

 What Do You Know?

 What Is Your Plan?

 Solve the Problem!

 Look Back and Explain!

Visualize It!

NAME: _____ **DATE:** _____

DIRECTIONS: Look at the example. Then, solve the problem.

Example: Use a bar model to subtract the numbers.

$$5 - 0.8 = \underline{4.2}$$

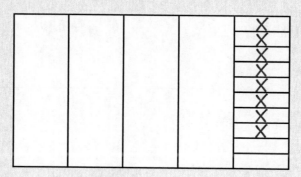

Use a bar model to subtract the numbers.

$$6 - 3.2 = \underline{\hphantom{XXXX}}$$

NAME: _____ DATE: _____

DIRECTIONS: Show two ways to solve the problem.

1. Hamad is buying an assortment of chocolate candies for his teacher at a candy store. He chooses 5.76 ounces of chocolate covered raisins, 3.2 ounces of chocolate caramels, and 5.15 ounces of chocolate raspberry creams. How many ounces of chocolate pretzels should he order if he wants to buy exactly 16 ounces of chocolate?

Strategy 1 . . . .

Strategy 2 . . . .

2. Which strategy do you like better? Explain your reasoning.

_____

_____

_____

_____

_____

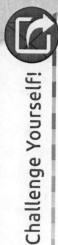

Challenge Yourself!

NAME: _____ **DATE:** _____

DIRECTIONS: Read and solve the problem.

Kristen's older sister begins the month with $100.00 in her checking account. She writes a check for her cell phone bill for $42.17. She uses her debit card at the gas station for $23.90. Then, she makes two more purchases using her debit card for $11.93 and $18.24.

1. How much money does Kristen spend during the month? Show how you found your answer.

2. How much money does Kristen have left? Show how you found your answer.

NAME: _____ DATE: _____

DIRECTIONS: Think about the problem, and answer the questions.

> Wade buys 5 gel pens. Each gel pen costs $0.73. How much money does Wade spend? Estimate, and then calculate the solution. Compare the solution to your estimate.

1. Will a reasonable estimate be greater than or less than $5.00? Explain your reasoning.

   _____

   _____

2. When Wade calculates the solution, he gets $36.50. He knows this is an unreasonable solution based on his estimate. How does he know this?

   _____

   _____

3. Wade decides to draw a picture to find the solution. He uses hundredths grids. How can Wade use his diagram to help him find the correct solution?

   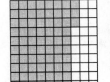  

   _____

   _____

   _____

Solve It!

NAME: _____ **DATE:** _____

DIRECTIONS: Read and solve each problem.

Problem 1: Wade buys 5 gel pens. Each gel pen costs $0.73. How much money does Wade spend? Estimate, and then calculate the solution. Compare the solution to your estimate.

 What Do You Know?

 What Is Your Plan?

 Solve the Problem!

 Look Back and Explain!

Problem 2: Wade buys 3 packs of markers. Each pack of markers costs $3.19. How much money does Wade spend? Estimate, and then calculate the solution. Compare the solution to your estimate.

 What Do You Know?

 What Is Your Plan?

 Solve the Problem!

 Look Back and Explain!

NAME: _____ **DATE:** _____

DIRECTIONS: Look at the example. Then, solve the problem.

Example: Elsa is cutting squares of paper for a project. Each square must measure 2.1 centimeters on each side. What is the area of one of the squares of paper?

2 groups of 2 = 4

2 groups of 0.1 = 0.2

2 groups of 0.1 = 0.2

1 group of 0.01 = 0.01

Total area = 4.41 square centimeters

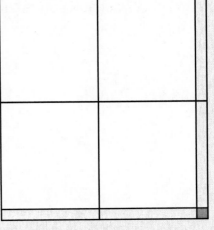

Elsa wants to put squares of paper in each corner of her poster board that measure 1.4 centimeters on each side. What is the area of one of the corner squares of paper?

_____ group of _____ = _____

_____ group of _____ = _____

_____ group of _____ = _____

_____ group of _____ = _____

Total area = _____ square centimeters

Solve It Two Ways!

NAME: _____ **DATE:** _____

DIRECTIONS: Show two ways to solve the problem.

1. A decimal point in each factor is missing in the equation below. Where can you place a decimal point in each factor to make the equation true? Show your work to prove your solution is correct.

$$43 \times 75 = 32.25$$

Strategy 1

Strategy 2

2. Which strategy do you like better? Explain your reasoning.

_____

_____

_____

_____

_____

Challenge Yourself!

NAME: _____ **DATE:** _____

 DIRECTIONS: Read and solve the problem.

Jorge takes a taxi while visiting New York City. The starting fare is $3.25. Then, the fare is an additional $2.25 per mile. There is also a charge of $0.30 for every minute spent sitting in traffic. The company calculates partial miles and minutes. Jorge travels 12.6 miles. He spends $3\frac{1}{2}$ minutes sitting in traffic. What is the total fare that Jorge must pay?

1. Write an expression that will help you solve the problem.

_____

2. How much does Jorge pay for his total taxi fare? Show your thinking.

Think About It!

NAME: _____   DATE: _____

 DIRECTIONS: Think about the problem, and answer the questions.

> Chloe buys 2.5 pounds of ground turkey. Her total bill is $8.85. What is the price per pound of ground turkey? Estimate, and then calculate the solution. Compare the solution to your estimate.

1. Chloe estimates she will spend $4.00 per pound. Do you think her estimate is greater than or less than the actual price per pound? Explain your reasoning.

_____

_____

_____

_____

2. Chloe's brother estimates Chloe will spend $3.00 per pound. Do you think his estimate is greater than or less than the actual price per pound? Explain your reasoning.

_____

_____

_____

_____

NAME: _____ DATE: _____

 DIRECTIONS: Read and solve each problem.

Problem 1: Chloe buys 2.5 pounds of ground turkey. Her total bill is $8.85. What is the price per pound of ground turkey? Estimate, and then calculate the solution. Compare the solution to your estimate.

 What Do You Know?

 What Is Your Plan?

 Solve the Problem!

 Look Back and Explain!

Problem 2: Chloe uses 2.5 pounds of ground turkey to make 10 meatballs. What is the weight in pounds of each meatball? Estimate, and then calculate the solution. Compare the solution to your estimate.

 What Do You Know?

 What Is Your Plan?

 Solve the Problem!

 Look Back and Explain!

Visualize It!

NAME: _____ **DATE:** _____

DIRECTIONS: Look at the example. Then, solve the problem.

Example: Adele works at a fudge shop. She needs to cut a large bar of chocolate fudge that is 1.2 meters long. Each piece must be 0.3 meters long. How many pieces of fudge will there be?

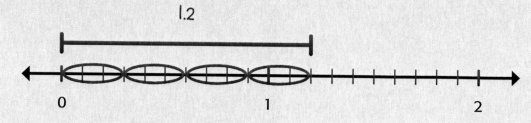

There are 4 groups of 0.3 in 1.2.

$1.2 \div 0.3 = 4$ pieces

Adele needs to cut a bar of rocky road fudge that is 0.8 meters long. Each piece must be 0.2 meters long. How many pieces of fudge will there be?

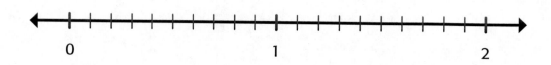

_____

_____

NAME: _____ DATE: _____

 DIRECTIONS: Show two ways to solve the problem.

1. What decimal number will make the equation true? Show your work to prove your solution is correct.

$$5 \div \text{_____} = 500$$

Strategy 1

· ·

Strategy 2

· ·

2. Which strategy do you prefer? Explain your reasoning.

_____

_____

_____

_____

_____

NAME: _____ DATE: _____

DIRECTIONS: Read and solve the problem.

Mr. Ly has a gift card to Coffee Express with a balance of $38.50. He orders the same items every time he goes there. His favorite drink costs $4.65 and a cookie costs $0.85. How many times can he buy his favorite drink and a cookie using his gift card?

1. How much does his favorite drink and a cookie cost? Explain how to find the answer.

_____

_____

_____

2. Show how to solve the problem.

NAME: _____ **DATE:** _____

DIRECTIONS: Think about the problem, and answer the questions.

> Austin goes on a field trip to the zoo with his fifth-grade class. The students see a gecko that measures 36 centimeters in length. They also see a salamander that measures 89 millimeters in length.

1. What question can Austin's teacher ask the class about the lengths of the gecko and the salamander?

   _____

   _____

   _____

2. Convert the following units:

   1 cm = _____ mm

   1 mm = _____ cm

   36 cm = _____ mm

   89 mm = _____ cm

NAME: _____ **DATE:** _____

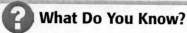 Read and solve each problem.

Solve It!

Problem 1: Austin goes on a field trip to the zoo with his fifth-grade class. The students see a gecko that measures 36 centimeters in length. They also see a salamander that measures 89 millimeters in length. The teacher asks the class, "Is the gecko or the salamander longer? How much longer?"

 What Do You Know?

 What Is Your Plan?

 Solve the Problem!

 Look Back and Explain!

Problem 2: Austin's class learns that an elephant drinks up to 200,000 milliliters of water a day. A thirsty camel drinks 135 liters of water. Which animal drinks more? How much more?

 What Do You Know?

 What Is Your Plan?

 Solve the Problem!

Look Back and Explain!

NAME: _____ DATE: _____

DIRECTIONS: Look at the example. Then, solve the problem.

Visualize It!

Example: A boa constrictor can reach a length of 3.9 meters. A python can measure 610 centimeters. Which snake is longer? How much longer?

Snake	Centimeters (cm)	Meters (m)
boa constrictor	390	3.9
python	610	6.1

The python is longer by 220 cm or 2.2 m.

An emperor penguin at the zoo weighs 23.13 kg. A macaroni penguin weighs 5,500 grams. Which penguin weighs more? How much more?

Penguin	Grams (g)	Kilograms (kg)
emperor penguin		23.13
macaroni penguin	5,500	

Solve It Two Ways!

NAME: _____ **DATE:** _____

DIRECTIONS: Show two ways to solve the problem.

1. An airplane has a wingspan of 3,596 centimeters and a length of 42.06 meters. Which is longer, the airplane's wingspan or its length? How much longer?

Strategy 1

Strategy 2

2. Which strategy do you think is easier? Explain your reasoning.

_____

_____

_____

_____

_____

NAME: _____ DATE: _____

DIRECTIONS: Read and solve the problem.

A zoo buys hay in bundles that each weigh 680 kilograms. Two elephants each eat 55,000 grams of hay per day.

1. How much hay do both elephants eat in one week? Show how you solved the problem.

2. Is one bundle of hay enough to feed both elephants for a week? Explain how you know.

_____

_____

_____

_____

_____

Think About It!

NAME: _____ **DATE:** _____

DIRECTIONS: Think about the problem, and answer the questions.

Mrs. Moore needs a new tile floor for her bathroom. She only wants four-sided tiles with all four sides equal in length. Name two shapes she can pick for the tiles. Draw a sketch and describe each tile.

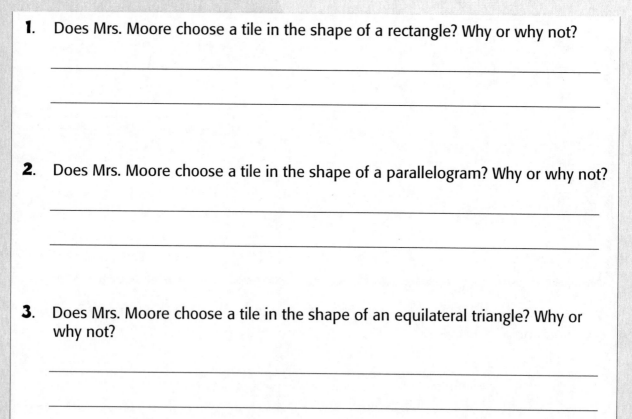

1. Does Mrs. Moore choose a tile in the shape of a rectangle? Why or why not?

_____

_____

2. Does Mrs. Moore choose a tile in the shape of a parallelogram? Why or why not?

_____

_____

3. Does Mrs. Moore choose a tile in the shape of an equilateral triangle? Why or why not?

_____

_____

NAME: _____ DATE: _____

 **DIRECTIONS:** Read and solve each problem.

Problem 1: Mrs. Moore needs a new tile floor for her bathroom. She only wants four-sided tiles with four sides that are equal in length. Name two shapes she can pick for the tiles. Draw a sketch and describe each tile.

 What Do You Know?

 What Is Your Plan?

 Solve the Problem!

 Look Back and Explain!

Problem 2: Mrs. Moore also needs new tiles for her kitchen. She only wants four-sided tiles with four equal angles. Name two shapes she can pick for the tiles. Draw a sketch and describe each tile.

 What Do You Know?

 What Is Your Plan?

 Solve the Problem!

 Look Back and Explain!

Visualize It!

NAME: _____ **DATE:** _____

DIRECTIONS: Look at the example. Then, solve the problem.

Example: Prove why the statement is *sometimes* true by writing examples and non-examples.

Sometimes a rectangle is a square.

Example	Non-example
• All 4 sides are equal • All 4 angles are equal • All 4 angles are 90 degrees • Opposite sides are parallel	• All 4 sides are not equal • No pairs of parallel sides

1. Prove why the statement is *sometimes* true by writing examples and non-examples.

Sometimes a parallelogram is a rhombus.

Example	Non-example

2. Write your own statement that is *sometimes* true. Then, complete the table by writing examples and non-examples.

_____

Example	Non-example

NAME: _____ **DATE:** _____

DIRECTIONS: Show two ways to solve the problem.

1. What changes, if any, would you need to make to a square to change it to a different shape? Sketch the new shape, and describe the changes you made.

Strategy 1

_____

_____

_____

Strategy 2

_____

_____

_____

2. Which shape was easier for you to make? Explain your reasoning.

_____

_____

_____

Challenge Yourself!

NAME: _____ **DATE:** _____

DIRECTIONS: Read and solve the problem.

Mr. Martinez tells his students that a kite is a special quadrilateral with two pairs of adjacent (touching) sides that are equal. He shows them two examples.

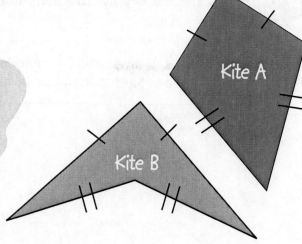

1. Draw a picture of two different quadrilaterals from the examples shown that are kites. Draw tick marks to show the quadrilaterals are kites.

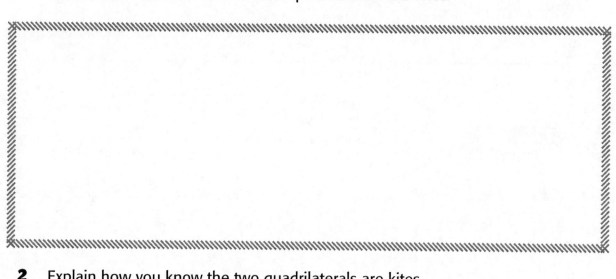

2. Explain how you know the two quadrilaterals are kites.

_____

_____

_____

3. How is Kite B different?

_____

_____

_____

NAME: _____ DATE: _____

 DIRECTIONS: Think about the problem, and answer the questions.

> A regular polygon is defined as a polygon with equal sides and equal angles. Which quadrilateral can be described as a regular polygon? How do you know?

1. List the quadrilaterals that have all equal sides. Draw a picture of each quadrilateral to show they have equal sides.

2. List the quadrilaterals that have all equal angles. Draw a picture of each quadrilateral to show they have equal angles.

3. Do any quadrilaterals appear on both lists? If so, write the names of the quadrilaterals that have all equal sides and all equal angles.

_____

_____

Solve It!

NAME: _____ **DATE:** _____

 **DIRECTIONS:** Read and solve each problem.

Problem 1: A regular polygon is defined as a polygon with all equal sides and all equal angles. Which quadrilateral can be described as a regular polygon? How do you know?

 What Do You Know?

 What Is Your Plan?

 Solve the Problem!

 Look Back and Explain!

Problem 2: What type of triangle can be described as a regular polygon? How do you know?

 What Do You Know?

 What Is Your Plan?

 Solve the Problem!

 Look Back and Explain!

NAME: _____ **DATE:** _____

 DIRECTIONS: Look at the example. Then, solve the problem.

Example: Use the Word Bank to write the names of the shapes in the chart.

Word Bank		
scalene	equilateral	isosceles

Triangles

3 equal sides	2 equal sides	no equal sides
equilateral	isosceles	scalene

Use the Word Bank to write the names of the shapes in the chart, including a title.

Word Bank		
kite	rhombus	rectangle
trapezoid	quadrilaterals	square

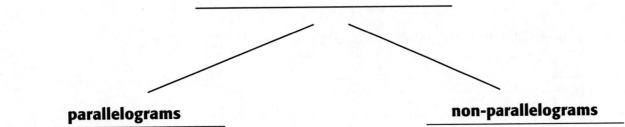

parallelograms   **non-parallelograms**

NAME: _____ **DATE:** _____

Solve It Two Ways!

DIRECTIONS: Show two ways to solve the problem.

1. Ling is drawing different types of triangles. She wants to draw two triangles each with one obtuse angle. Draw an obtuse scalene triangle and an obtuse isosceles triangle.

· · · · Obtuse scalene triangle ·

· · · · Obtuse isosceles triangle ·

2. Is it possible to draw an obtuse equilateral triangle? Why or why not?

_____

_____

_____

_____

_____

_____

© Shell Education

NAME: _____ **DATE:** _____

DIRECTIONS: Read and solve the problem.

Juan and Akoni are playing the Quadrilateral Properties game. They earn 1 point for each property that describes a quadrilateral they draw.

Quadrilateral Properties

- all sides equal
- all angles equal
- two pairs of parallel sides
- opposite sides equal
- adjacent (touching) sides equal

1. Draw quadrilaterals worth 5 points, 4 points, 3 points, 2 points, and 1 point each. Label how many points each is worth.

2. Explain how you know the score for each quadrilateral is correct.

_____

_____

_____

3. Is it possible to draw a quadrilateral worth 0 points? Explain your reasoning.

_____

_____

Think About It!

NAME: _____ DATE: _____

DIRECTIONS: Think about the problem, and answer the questions.

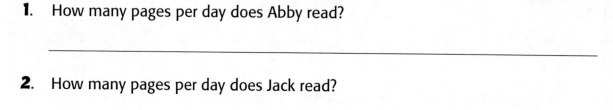

Abby and Jack read the same amount of pages of their books each day. How many pages do Abby and Jack read after 4 days? Complete the table to show the patterns.

Day	Abby's pages read	Jack's pages read
0	0	0
1	3	6
2	6	12
3		
4		

1. How many pages per day does Abby read?

   _____

2. How many pages per day does Jack read?

   _____

3. How many times greater is Jack's number of pages on each day than Abby's number of pages? Explain how you know.

   _____

   _____

   _____

   _____

NAME: _____ **DATE:** _____

 DIRECTIONS: Read and solve each problem.

Problem 1: Abby and Jack read the same amount of pages of their books each day. How many pages do Abby and Jack read after 4 days? Complete the table to show the patterns.

Day	Abby's pages read	Jack's pages read
0	0	0
1	3	6
2	6	12
3		
4		

 What Do You Know?

 What Is Your Plan?

 Solve the Problem!

 Look Back and Explain!

Problem 2: Henry and Jane also read the same amount of pages in their books each day. How many pages do Henry and Jane read after 4 days? Complete the table to show the patterns.

Day	Henry's pages read	Jane's pages read
0	0	0
1	5	10
2		
3	15	
4		

 What Do You Know?

 What Is Your Plan?

 Solve the Problem!

 Look Back and Explain!

NAME: _____   **DATE:** _____

Visualize It!

DIRECTIONS: Look at the example. Then, solve the problem.

Example: David and Dana feed their betta fish the same number of food pellets each day. Complete the table to see how many pellets each betta fish eats in a week. Graph the ordered pairs on the coordinate plane.

Day	Food pellets eaten by David's betta fish	Food pellets eaten by Dana's betta fish
0	0	0
1	2	4
2	4	8
3	6	12
4	8	16
5	10	20
6	12	24
7	14	28

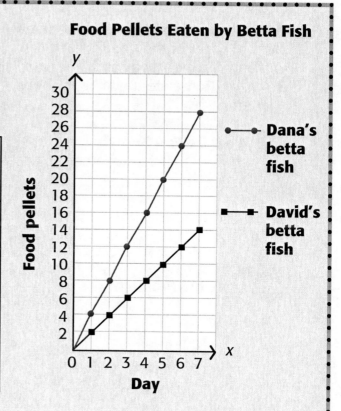

Food Pellets Eaten by Betta Fish

- Dana's betta fish
- David's betta fish

Gordon and Lexie feed their turtles the same number of food pellets each day. Complete the table to see how many pellets each turtle eats in a week. Graph the ordered pairs on the coordinate plane.

Day	Food pellets eaten by Gordon's turtle	Food pellets eaten by Lexie's turtle
0	0	0
1	4	8
2	8	16
3		
4		
5		
6		
7		

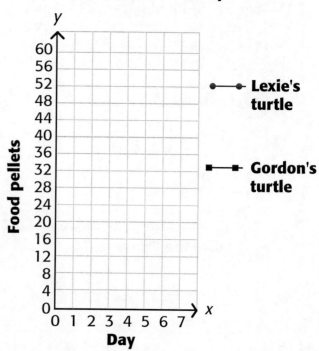

Food Pellets Eaten by Turtles

- Lexie's turtle
- Gordon's turtle

NAME: _____ DATE: _____

 DIRECTIONS: Show two ways to present the data.

1. Clay and Cameron track the video game levels they pass each day. Clay uses a table, and Cameron uses a graph. Plot Clay's data from the table onto the graph. Record Cameron's data from the graph into the table.

······· Clay's Table ·············· ···· Cameron's Graph ···········

Day	Clay's levels passed	Cameron's levels passed
0	0	0
1	3	
2	6	
3	9	
4	12	
5	15	
6	18	
7	21	

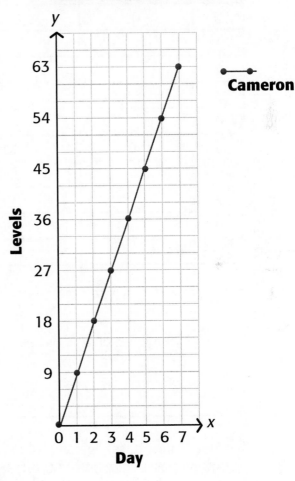

Video Game Levels Passed

Cameron

2. Do you prefer to present data in a table or a graph? Explain your reasoning.

_____

_____

_____

Challenge Yourself!

NAME: _____ **DATE:** _____

DIRECTIONS: Read and solve the problem.

At an amusement park, there is a Kids Minifun Coaster and a Giant Racer Coaster. Complete the table to show the total number of passengers for both coasters. Graph the data on the coordinate plane. Then, answer the questions.

Coaster rides	Passengers on Kids Minifun Coaster	Passengers on Giant Racer Coaster
0	0	0
1		
2		
3		
4		
5	50	100
6		
7		
8		
9		
10		

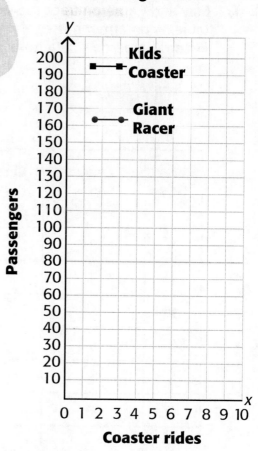

Passengers Carried

1. How many passengers did each coaster carry after 10 rides?

_____

_____

2. How many passengers would each coaster have carried after 20 rides? How many passengers after 60 rides?

_____

_____

3. Based on the information, how many passengers can ride each coaster at a time? How do you know?

_____

_____

NAME: _____ **DATE:** _____

DIRECTIONS: Think about the problem, and answer the questions.

Plot the points on the coordinate plane, and connect them in order. Connect point D back to point A. What shape is formed?

A (2, 1)   B (4, 1)
C (6, 4)   D (0, 4)

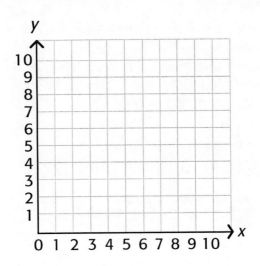

Think About It!

1. How many sides do you predict the shape will have? Explain your reasoning.

_____

_____

2. Rewrite the points in the table.

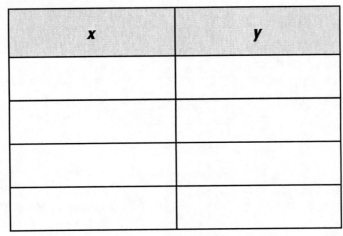

x	y

3. Does the order of the x- and y-coordinates matter? Why or why not?

_____

_____

_____

NAME: _____ **DATE:** _____

 DIRECTIONS: Read and solve each problem.

Problem 1: Plot the points on the coordinate plane. Connect them in order. Connect point D back to point A. What shape is formed?

A (2, 1)   B (4, 1)
C (6, 4)   D (0, 4)

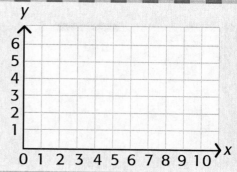

? What Do You Know?

What Is Your Plan?

Solve the Problem!

Look Back and Explain!

Problem 2: Plot the points on the coordinate plane. Connect them in order. Connect the last point back to the first point. What shape is formed?

x	y
2	1
6	1
2	6

? What Do You Know?

What Is Your Plan?

Solve the Problem!

Look Back and Explain!

NAME: _____ DATE: _____

 DIRECTIONS: Look at the example. Then, solve the problem.

Example: Draw a line segment from (2, 2) to (6, 4). What points can you use to draw another line segment that is parallel to this one? Plot your points to prove your solution is correct.

Solution: <u>(2, 0) and (6, 2)</u>

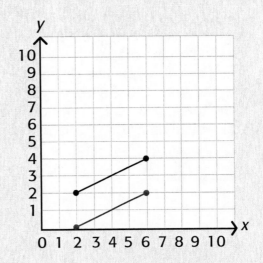

1. Draw a line segment from (1, 6) to (6, 5). What points can you use to draw another line segment that is parallel to this one? Plot your points to prove your solution is correct.

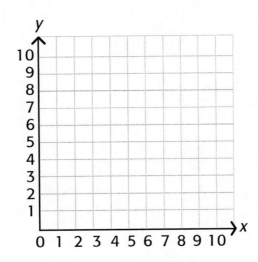

   Solution: _____

2. Can there be more than one correct solution? Explain your reasoning.

   _____

   _____

   _____

Solve It Two Ways!

NAME: _____ DATE: _____

 DIRECTIONS: Show two ways to solve the problem.

1. The locations of a playground and a frozen yogurt shop on a map are shown. Label each location on the map with the correct ordered pair. Then, describe two different paths from the playground to the frozen yogurt shop using the grid lines. Explain how many units you moved up or down and left or right.

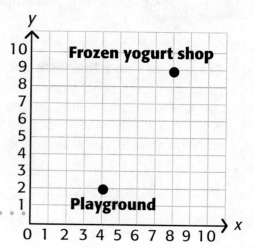

Path 1

Path 2

2. Is one path better than the other? Explain your reasoning.

_____

_____

_____

NAME: _____ **DATE:** _____

DIRECTIONS: Read and solve the problem.

Wendell the Worm is a character in a new video game. Plot the points on the coordinate plane and connect them to find out what Wendell looks like in Level A.

Level A

x	y
1	1
2	1
2	5
1	5

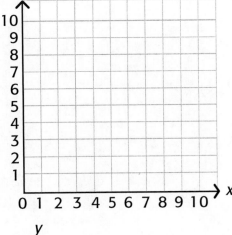

1. Wendell looks different in Level B. The x-coordinate is multiplied by 2, but the y-coordinate stays the same as in Level A. Complete the Level B table and plot the points on the coordinate plane. How does Wendell look different in Level B than in Level A?

Level B

x	y

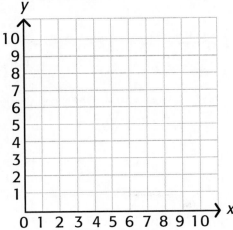

_____

_____

2. Wendell looks different in Level C. The x-coordinate stays the same as in Level A, but the y-coordinate is multiplied by 2. Complete the Level C table, and plot the points on the coordinate plane. How does Wendell look different in Level C than in Level A?

Level C

x	y

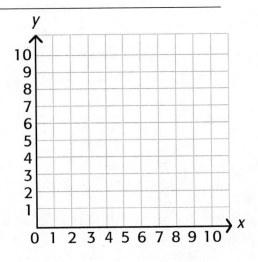

_____

_____

Think About It!

NAME: _____ **DATE:** _____

DIRECTIONS: Think about the problem, and answer the questions.

Plot and connect the points to form a line segment. What points can you add to the line segment to make a parallelogram? Draw a parallelogram on the coordinate plane.

A (3, 2)   B (1, 5)

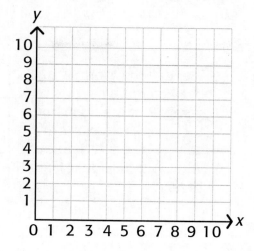

1. How many more points will you need to make a parallelogram? How do you know?

_____

_____

_____

2. Is there more than one way to solve the problem?

_____

_____

_____

3. What do you know about the sides and angles of a parallelogram?

_____

_____

_____

NAME: _____ **DATE:** _____

 Read and solve each problem.

Problem 1: Plot and connect the points to form a line segment. What points can you add to the line segment to make a parallelogram? Draw a parallelogram on the coordinate plane.

A (3, 2)　　　B (1, 5)

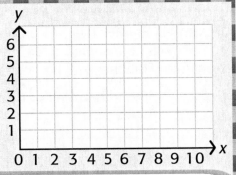

 What Do You Know?

What Is Your Plan?

 Solve the Problem!

Look Back and Explain!

Problem 2: Plot and connect the points to form a line segment. What point can you add to the line segment to make a triangle? Draw a triangle on the coordinate plane.

A (3, 2)　　　B (1, 5)

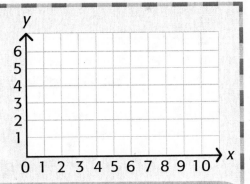

 What Do You Know?

What Is Your Plan?

 Solve the Problem!

Look Back and Explain!

Solve It!

Visualize It!

NAME: _____ DATE: _____

DIRECTIONS: Look at the example. Then, solve the problem.

Example: Bradley has $45 on his school lunch card. Each lunch costs $4. How much money will he have left after 5 lunches? How much money after 10 lunches? After how many lunches will he need to put more money on his card?

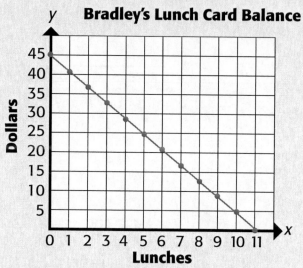

Bradley's Lunch Card Balance

Lunches	Dollars
0	45
1	41
2	37
3	33
4	29
5	25
6	21
7	17
8	13
9	9
10	5
11	1

Bradley has $25 left after 5 lunches. He has $5 left after 10 lunches. He will need to put more money on his card after 11 lunches.

Jennifer has $25 on a frozen yogurt gift card. Her favorite frozen yogurt costs $3. How much money does she have left after 3 frozen yogurts? How much money after 6 frozen yogurts? After how many frozen yogurts will she need to put more money on her card?

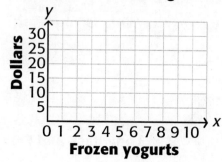

Jennifer's Frozen Yogurt Card

Frozen yogurts	Dollars

_____

_____

#51617—180 Days of Problem Solving

NAME: _____ DATE: _____

DIRECTIONS: Show two ways to solve the problem.

1. Plot and connect the points (5, 1) and (5, 4) to make a line segment. Add more points to make two different rectangles each with a perimeter of 10 units.

 Rectangle 1

 Rectangle 2

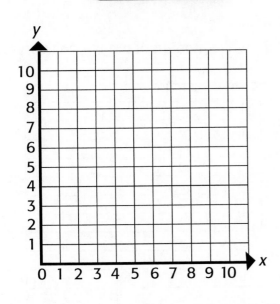

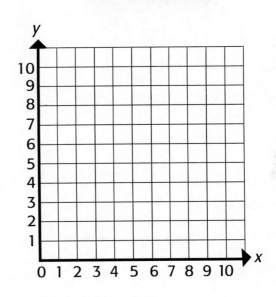

2. What information about each rectangle did you know after making the line segment? How did you determine what other points to add to make the perimeter of each rectangle 10 units?

_____

_____

_____

_____

_____

_____

_____

Challenge Yourself!

NAME: _____ **DATE:** _____

DIRECTIONS: Read and solve the problem.

Violet has a summer job as a clerk at a public library. She earns $7 per hour. She is saving for a skateboard that costs $110. She already has $20 saved. If she saves all of her money, how many hours will she need to work to buy the skateboard?

1. Complete the table and make a graph to show the amount of money Violet saves.

Hours worked (x)	Dollars saved (y)

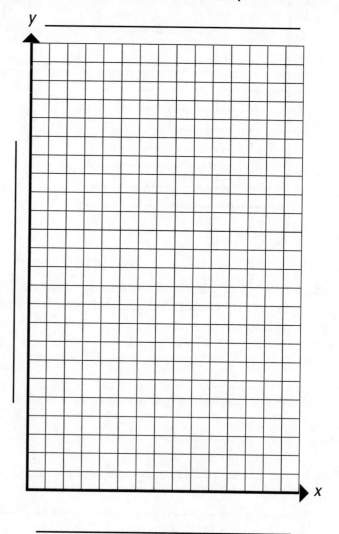

2. How many hours does Violet need to work to buy the skateboard? Explain how you know.

_____

_____

ANSWER KEY

Week 1: Day 1 (page 13)

1. The number of zeros in the product is the same, as the power of 10. 38×10^5 has two digits for the base number and five digits for the zeros, for a total of seven digits.

2. Yes, the number of digits would change. Only four zeros would appear in the product, so there would be a total of six digits.

3. Marsha would need six blanks for the digits: one blank for the base number and five for the zeros.

Week 1: Day 2 (page 14)

1. 3,800,000; 38 is the base number and the power of 10 is 5; write 38 and five zeros

2. 30,000; 3 is the base number and the power of 10 is 4; write 3 and four zeros

Week 1: Day 3 (page 15)

1. Answers will vary due to selection of base number, but should follow this framework:

Exponent form	Expanded form	Expression	Standard form
___ $\times 10^1$	___ $\times$ 10	___ $\times$ 10	___0
___ $\times 10^2$	___ $\times$ 10 $\times$ 10	___ $\times$ 100	___00
___ $\times 10^3$	___ $\times$ 10 $\times$ 10 $\times$ 10	___ $\times$ 1,000	___,000
___ $\times 10^4$	___ $\times$ 10 $\times$ 10 $\times$ 10 $\times$ 10	___ $\times$ 10,000	___0,000
___ $\times 10^5$	___ $\times$ 10 $\times$ 10 $\times$ 10 $\times$ 10 $\times$ 10	___ $\times$ 100,000	___00,000
___ $\times 10^6$	___ $\times$ 10 $\times$ 10 $\times$ 10 $\times$ 10 $\times$ 10 $\times$ 10	___ $\times$ 1,000,000	___,000,000

2. The number of tens in the expanded form is the same as the exponent. The number of zeros in the product is the same as the exponent.

Week 1: Day 4 (page 16)

1. Possible answers: 14,000,000 and $14 \times 10 \times 10 \times 10 \times 10 \times 10 \times 10$

2. Possible answer: I think writing the standard form of a number is the best way to write the results because it gives a total amount without any calculations necessary.

Week 1: Day 5 (page 17)

1. $2 \times (37 \times 10^4) = 74 \times 10^4 = 740{,}000$ km

2. 3 round trips; Possible explanation: One round trip is 740,000 kilometers. There are 3 groups of 740,000 in 2,220,000, so she made 3 round trips.

Week 2: Day 1 (page 18)

1. The first step in the teacher's problem is $12 + 8$ because it is in parentheses.

2. The first step in the problem Katy wrote would be 15×12 because there are no parentheses, and multiplication comes before addition in the order of operations.

3. No, parentheses in a problem change the order in which a problem is solved and the answer.

Week 2: Day 2 (page 19)

1. No; The answer to Mrs. Johnson's problem is 300. The answer to Katy's problem is 188.

2. No; The answer to Mrs. Johnson's problem is 83. The answer to Katy's problem is 67.

Week 2: Day 3 (page 20)

1.

Expression with no grouping symbols	Expression with grouping symbols
	$5 \times \{2 \times [(6-3) \times 4 + 8]\} + 10^3$
	$5 \times \{2 \times [3 \times 4 + 8]\} + 10^3$
$5 \times 2 \times 6 - 3 \times 4 + 8 + 10^3$	$5 \times \{2 \times [12 + 8]\} + 10^3$
$5 \times 2 \times 6 - 3 \times 4 + 8 + 1{,}000$	$5 \times \{2 \times 20\} + 10^3$
$60 - 12 + 8 + 1{,}000$	$5 \times 40 + 10^3$
$1{,}056$	$5 \times 40 + 1{,}000$
	$200 + 1{,}000$
	$1{,}200$

2. Possible answer: No, grouping symbols change the order in which the calculations are performed. If there are no grouping symbols, the order of operations follows this order: exponents, multiply or divide from left to right, and add or subtract from left to right.

ANSWER KEY (cont.)

Week 2: Day 4 (page 21)

1. Possible answers: $(5 + 4) \times 9 \div 3 + 7 = 34$; $5 + 4 \times (9 \div 3 + 7) = 45$

2. Possible answer: I used guess and check with grouping symbols, different combinations of numbers, and the order of operations to make the statements true.

Week 2: Day 5 (page 22)

1. Possible equations: $1 + 2 + 3 + 4 = 10$; $(1 \times 2 \times 3) + 4 = 10$; $(4 \times 3) - (2 \times 1) = 10$; $4 \times 2 + 3 - 1 = 10$; $3 \times 2 + 4 \times 1 = 10$; $4 \times 3 - 2 \div 1 = 10$; $4 \div 1 \times 3 - 2 = 10$

2. Possible answer: I used guess and check with grouping symbols, different combinations of numbers, and the order of operations to find different equations with a solution of 10.

Week 3: Day 1 (page 23)

1. Possible answers: 5 times 7; 5 groups of 7; 5 rows of 7

2. Possible answers: 10 times the product of 5 and 7; 10 times the amount of 5 times 7

3. $10(5 \times 7)$ will have a greater solution because it is 10 times greater than 5×7.

Week 3: Day 2 (page 24)

1. The expressions are related by a factor of 10. The expression $10(5 \times 7)$ is ten times greater than 5×7. There are ten groups of 5×7.

2. The expressions are related by a factor of 3. The expression $3 \times (120 + 25)$ is three times greater than $120 + 25$. There are 3 groups of $120 + 25$.

Week 3: Day 3 (page 25)

1.

Description	Expression
Triple 18 and add 12.	$3 \times 18 + 12$
Divide 45 and 5. Subtract 2 from the quotient.	$45 \div 5 - 2$
Find the quotient of 72 and 8. Multiply the quotient by 6.	$6(72 \div 8)$
Find the sum of 21 and 15. Find the quotient of the sum and 3.	$(21 + 15) \div 3$

2. Possible answer: The important words are *sum*, *difference*, *product*, and *quotient*, which indicate the operation. Words like *double* and *triple* tell what to multiply by.

Week 3: Day 4 (page 26)

1. In Strategy 1, both expressions are correct ways of writing the description. In both cases, the solution is 34. In Strategy 2, $(2 \times 10) - 14$ is a correct representation of the description, but $14 - (2 \times 10)$ is not. The solution to the first expression is 6, but the second expression results in $14 - 20$, which is not equal to 6.

2. Possible answer: The order of numbers and operations signs matter in subtraction and division, but not in addition and multiplication.

Week 3: Day 5 (page 27)

1. Possible answer: $3(500 + 750 - 200)$

2. Possible answer: $(500 + 750 - 200) + (500 + 750 - 200) + (500 + 750 - 200)$

3. Student answers will vary, but the two different expressions for the total score should reflect the amount of points scored in 3 rounds.

Week 4: Day 1 (page 28)

1. A bookstore ordered 175 dozen pencils. There are 12 pencils in a dozen.

2. Possible answer: Since there are 12 pencils in one dozen, I can multiply 175 by 12 to solve the problem.

3. Possible answer: I can solve the problem a different way by adding 12 groups of 175.

Week 4: Day 2 (page 29)

1. 2,100 pencils; multiply 175 by 12

2. 900 erasers; multiply 36 by 25

Week 4: Day 3 (page 30)

1. $40,000 + 2,400 + 560 + 4,500 + 270 + 63 = 47,793$

$\times$	500	30	7
80	40,000	2,400	560
9	4,500	270	63

2. Possible answer: The model helps me solve the problem because breaking down (decomposing) the number by place value makes the multiplication easier to do.

Week 4: Day 4 (page 31)

1. 8,592 bags of popcorn; Possible strategies: multiplication; repeated addition; picture; area model

2. Possible answer: I think drawing an area model is better because it helps me to organize all of the partial products.

ANSWER KEY *(cont.)*

Week 4: Day 5 (page 32)

1. Greatest possible product:
   $965 \times 87 = 83,955$

2. Possible explanation: Since I wanted the greatest product, I wrote the greater digits in the bigger place values.

Week 5: Day 1 (page 33)

1. There are 1,572 students. They need to be placed in groups of 14.

2. There will be more than 100 groups because 100×14 is 1,400, and there are more than 1,400 students at Central Middle School.

Week 5: Day 2 (page 34)

1. 112 groups; 4 students leftover; divide 1,572 by 14; the remainder will be how many students are left over.

2. 117 groups; 0 leftover; divide 936 by 8; the remainder will be how many students are left over.

Week 5: Day 3 (page 35)

1. $8,227 \div 72 = 114$ r.19; $100 + 10 + 4 = 114$; 114, remainder 19

	100	10	4
72	$100 \times 72 = 7,200$	$10 \times 72 = 720$	$4 \times 72 = 288$
	$8,227 - 7,200 = 1,027$	$1,027 - 720 = 307$	$307 - 288 =$ (19)

2. Possible answer: The model helps me solve the problem because using multiplication makes division easier for me.

Week 5: Day 4 (page 36)

1. 212 packages of paper; Possible strategies: division; repeated subtraction; picture; area model

2. Possible answer: I like drawing an area model because it helps me to organize all of the partial products.

Week 5: Day 5 (page 37)

1. Possible answer: Both vans will make 20 trips (large van: $25 \times 20 = 500$; small van: $15 \times 20 = 300$; $500 + 300 = 800$).

2. Possible answer: The large van will make 23 trips ($25 \times 23 = 575$). The small van will make 15 trips ($15 \times 15 = 225$). Both vans will transport 800 boxes ($575 + 225 = 800$).

3. Possible answer: I think if both vans make 20 trips that will be faster than if the large van makes 23 trips and the smaller van makes 15 trips.

Week 6: Day 1 (page 38)

1. 2 layers

2. 12 cubes

3. Possible answer: I can find the volume by counting the number of unit cubes in one layer and then multiplying the answer by the number of layers.

Week 6: Day 2 (page 39)

1. Amy is correct; figure has 2 layers of 12 unit cubes, which is 24 unit cubes; count the number of cubes in one layer and multiply by the number of layers.

2. Hector is correct; figure has 5 layers of 8 unit cubes, which is 40 unit cubes; count the number of cubes in one layer and multiply by the number of layers.

Week 6: Day 3 (page 40)

1.

Figure	Base layer	Number of layers	Total number of unit cubes
	2 cubic units	5	10

2. Possible answer: I can multiply the number of layers by the number of cubes in each layer, so I don't have to count all of the individual cubes.

ANSWER KEY *(cont.)*

Week 6: Day 4 (page 41)

1. Possible solutions: $1 \times 1 \times 8$; $1 \times 2 \times 4$; $2 \times 2 \times 2$.

2. Possible answer: I recommend the 2 inch $\times$ 2 inch $\times$ 2 inch package because it is a perfect cube and it will be easier to package the caramels.

Week 6: Day 5 (page 42)

1. Possible dimensions of box: $1 \times 1 \times 24$; $1 \times 2 \times 12$; $1 \times 3 \times 8$; $1 \times 4 \times 6$; $2 \times 6 \times 2$; and $2 \times 3 \times 4$; All designs should indicate the number of layers and number of cubic feet in each layer to show a total of 24 cubic feet.

2. Possible answer: I recommend the company use the 2 foot $\times$ 3 foot $\times$ 4 foot box because the box is wider and will be easier to package the basketballs.

Week 7: Day 1 (page 43)

1. The gift box is 8 centimeters long, 8 centimeters wide, and 2 centimeters high. It has a volume of 128 cubic centimeters. The second gift box is the same width, but twice the length, and three times the height.

2. The question is asking for the volume of the second box.

3. The answer cannot be 128 cubic centimeters because although the length is staying the same, the other dimensions are increasing. The volume will increase as well.

Week 7: Day 2 (page 44)

1. 768 cubic centimeters; dimensions of the gift box is $16 \times 8 \times 6$

2. 60 cubic feet; dimensions of second tool chest is $10 \times 3 \times 2$

Week 7: Day 3 (page 45)

1.

Sketch	Dimensions length × width × height	Volume
4 2 3	$2 \times 3 \times 4$	24 cubic units
2 3 4	$3 \times 4 \times 2$	24 cubic units

2. The order the dimensions does not change the volume because numbers can be multiplied in any order.

Week 7: Day 4 (page 46)

1. Possible solutions: $1 \times 1 \times 36$; $1 \times 2 \times 18$; $1 \times 3 \times 12$; $1 \times 4 \times 9$; $1 \times 6 \times 6$; $2 \times 2 \times 9$; $2 \times 3 \times 6$; $3 \times 3 \times 4$

2. Yes, there are several other solutions to this problem because there are many ways to multiply three dimensions with the solution of 36 cubic inches.

Week 7: Day 5 (page 47)

1. $30 \times 10 \times 8 = 2{,}400$ cubic centimeters

2. Dimensions of the bird feeder should have a volume of 4,800 cubic centimeters. Possible solution: $60 \times 10 \times 8$

3. Other possible solutions: $30 \times 40 \times 4$ and $30 \times 20 \times 8$

Week 8: Day 1 (page 48)

1. Multiplying all of the given side lengths will not result in the volume. The figure is made up of more than one rectangular prism.

2. Possible answer: $3 \times 4 \times 4$ and $3 \times 4 \times 2$

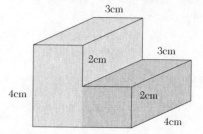

ANSWER KEY *(cont.)*

Week 8: Day 2 (page 49)

1. 72 cubic cm; $3 \times 4 \times 4 = 48$; $3 \times 4 \times 2 = 24$; $48 + 24 = 72$

2. 115 cubic in.; $5 \times 5 \times 1 = 25$; $6 \times 5 \times 3 = 90$; $25 + 90 = 115$

Week 8: Day 3 (page 50)

1.

Figure	Prism 1 dimensions and volume	Prism 2 dimensions and volume	Total volume
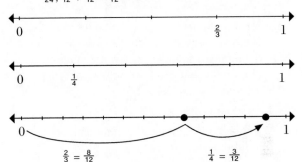	$1 \times 2 \times 6$ = 12 cubic feet	$8 \times 3 \times 3$ = 72 cubic feet	12 + 72 = 84 cubic feet

2. Finding two separate rectangular prisms allows you to find the volume of each, and then add the volumes together to get the total volume.

Week 8: Day 4 (page 51)

1. Volume of figure is 350 cubic meters; Possible dimensions: $7 \times 7 \times 5$ and $5 \times 3 \times 7$, or a $5 \times 7 \times 2$ and $5 \times 8 \times 7$.

2. Possible answer: I found the total volume of the figure by finding the volume of the figure by finding the volume of each prism, and then I added the volumes together.

Week 8: Day 5 (page 52)

1. Designs will vary, but should total 500 cubic feet; Possible answer: 10 feet × 5 feet × 5 feet and 25 feet × 5 feet × 2 feet

2. Possible answer: $(10 \times 5 \times 5) + (25 \times 5 \times 2) = 250 + 250 = 500$ cubic feet

3. Possible answers: $(8 \times 5 \times 5) + (10 \times 10 \times 3) = 200 + 300 = 500$ cubic feet; $(5 \times 4 \times 10) + (15 \times 2 \times 10) = 200 + 300 = 500$ cubic feet

Week 9: Day 1 (page 53)

1. B and D

2. $\frac{1}{3}$ is equal to $\frac{9}{27}$ (multiplied by $\frac{3}{3}$); $\frac{1}{3}$ is equal to $\frac{9}{27}$ (multiplied by $\frac{9}{9}$); $\frac{4}{9}$ is equal to $\frac{12}{27}$ (multiplied by $\frac{3}{3}$)

3. Possible answer: I would use $\frac{3}{9}$ and $\frac{4}{9}$ because 9 is the least common denominator of 3 and 9.

Week 9: Day 2 (page 54)

1. $\frac{7}{9}$ or $\frac{21}{27}$ cup, or any other equivalent fraction; add fractions; $\frac{1}{3} + \frac{4}{9} = \frac{3}{9} + \frac{4}{9} = \frac{7}{9}$

2. $\frac{5}{8}$ or $\frac{20}{32}$ cup, or any other equivalent fraction; add fractions; $\frac{1}{4} + \frac{3}{8} = \frac{2}{8} + \frac{3}{8} = \frac{5}{8}$

Week 9: Day 3 (page 55)

$\frac{11}{24}$; $\frac{8}{12} + \frac{3}{12} = \frac{11}{12}$

Week 9: Day 4 (page 56)

1. Possible problems: $1\frac{1}{12} + 2\frac{2}{3} = 3\frac{9}{12}$; $1\frac{1}{6} + 2\frac{7}{12} = 3\frac{9}{12}$; $1\frac{1}{4} + 2\frac{1}{2} = 3\frac{9}{12}$; $1\frac{1}{3} + 2\frac{5}{12} = 3\frac{9}{12}$

2. Possible answer: I think $1\frac{1}{12} + 2\frac{2}{3}$ is easier to solve because I know the common denominator for 12 and 3 is 12.

Week 9: Day 5 (page 57)

1. Models will vary, but should show the fractions being added together; Possible models: fraction model, number line; equations

2. $1\frac{1}{5} + \frac{1}{3} + \frac{1}{6} = 1\frac{6}{30} + \frac{10}{30} + \frac{5}{30} = 1\frac{21}{30}$ or $1\frac{7}{10}$ cups

Week 10: Day 1 (page 58)

1. A and D

2. $\frac{4}{5}$ is equal to $\frac{8}{10}$ (multiplied by $\frac{2}{2}$); $\frac{4}{5}$ is equal to $\frac{40}{50}$ (multiplied by $\frac{10}{10}$); $\frac{3}{10}$ is equal to $\frac{15}{50}$ (multiplied by $\frac{5}{5}$)

3. Possible answer: I would use $\frac{8}{10}$ and $\frac{3}{10}$ because 10 is the least common denominator of 5 and 10.

Week 10: Day 2 (page 59)

1. $\frac{5}{10}$, $\frac{1}{2}$, $\frac{25}{50}$, or any other equivalent fraction; subtract fractions; $\frac{4}{5} - \frac{3}{10} = \frac{8}{10} - \frac{3}{10} = \frac{5}{10}$ or $\frac{1}{2}$

2. $\frac{4}{12}$, $\frac{1}{3}$, $\frac{16}{48}$, or any other equivalent fraction; subtract fractions; $\frac{3}{4} - \frac{5}{12} = \frac{9}{12} - \frac{5}{12} = \frac{4}{12}$ or $\frac{1}{3}$

ANSWER KEY *(cont.)*

Week 10: Day 3 (page 60)

1. $1\frac{5}{6} - \frac{1}{2} = 1\frac{10}{12} - \frac{6}{12} = 1\frac{4}{12}$ or $1\frac{1}{3}$

2. A common denominator can be found for the fractions by multiplying the two denominators, finding a common multiple of both denominators, or finding the least common denominator.

Week 10: Day 4 (page 61)

1. $\frac{3}{8}$ mile; Possible strategies: fraction model; number line; equations; $\frac{3}{8} + \frac{1}{4} = \frac{3}{8} + \frac{2}{8} = \frac{5}{8}, \frac{8}{8} - \frac{5}{8} = \frac{3}{8}$

2. Possible answer: I think making a fraction model is easier because it helps me visualize the problem.

Week 10: Day 5 (page 62)

1. Possible models: fraction model, number line

2. Sammi Sloth, $\frac{5}{6} > \frac{2}{3}$ or $\frac{5}{6} > \frac{4}{6}$; $\frac{5}{6} - \frac{2}{3} = \frac{5}{6} - \frac{4}{6} = \frac{1}{6}$ longer

3. 4 hours; $\frac{1}{6}$ of one day, or 24 hours, is 4 hours

Week 11: Day 1 (page 63)

1. Jeff has $\frac{1}{8}$ bag of marshmallows. Annie has $\frac{1}{3}$ bag of marshmallows.

2. The solution will be less than 1 because both fractions are less than $\frac{1}{2}$.

3. Possible answer: I would choose 24 as a common denominator because 24 is a multiple of both 3 and 8.

Week 11: Day 2 (page 64)

1. $\frac{11}{24}$ bag of marshmallows; add fractions; $\frac{1}{8} + \frac{1}{3} = \frac{3}{24} + \frac{8}{24} = \frac{11}{24}$

2. $2\frac{1}{4}$ cups of trail mix is left; subtract fractions; $3\frac{3}{4} - 1\frac{1}{2} = 3\frac{3}{4} - 1\frac{2}{4} = 2\frac{1}{4}$

Week 11: Day 3 (page 65)

Yes, the ingredients will fit in the bowl because $2\frac{3}{6}$ or $2\frac{1}{2}$ is less than 3; $2\frac{3}{6}$ or $2\frac{1}{2}$ cups of ingredients; $1\frac{5}{6} + \frac{2}{3} = 1\frac{5}{6} + \frac{4}{6} = 1\frac{9}{6} = 2\frac{3}{6}$ or $2\frac{1}{2}$

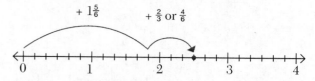

Week 11: Day 4 (page 66)

1. No; Possible strategies: fraction model, number line, equations; $\frac{1}{3} + \frac{3}{5} = \frac{5}{15} + \frac{9}{15} = \frac{14}{15}$; $\frac{14}{15} < \frac{15}{15}$ or 1

2. Possible answer: I like using equations because I can add the fractions by finding a common denominator and then compare my sum to 1 whole.

Week 11: Day 5 (page 67)

1. Answers will vary, but should show the fractions being subtracted; Possible answer: $1\frac{1}{5} - \frac{3}{10} = 1\frac{2}{10} - \frac{3}{10} = \frac{12}{10} - \frac{3}{10} = \frac{9}{10}$

2. $1\frac{1}{5} + \frac{3}{10} = 1\frac{2}{10} + \frac{3}{10} = 1\frac{5}{10}$ or $1\frac{1}{2}$

Week 12: Day 1 (page 68)

1. Each friend will get more than one brownie because four brownies are shared among 3 friends. Each friend will get one whole brownie and a part of another brownie.

2. 4 divided by 3, 4 ÷ 3, or $\frac{4}{3}$

Week 12: Day 2 (page 69)

1. $\frac{4}{3}$ or $1\frac{1}{3}$ brownies; write a division expression and divide; $4 ÷ 3 = \frac{4}{3} = 1\frac{1}{3}$

2. $\frac{4}{12}$ or $\frac{1}{3}$ of a box; write a division expression and simplify the fraction; $4 ÷ 12 = \frac{4}{12} = \frac{1}{3}$

Week 12: Day 3 (page 70)

$\frac{1}{6} + \frac{1}{6} + \frac{1}{6} + \frac{1}{6} + \frac{1}{6} + \frac{1}{6} + \frac{1}{6} + \frac{1}{6} = \frac{8}{6}$; $8 ÷ 6 = 1\frac{2}{6}$ or $1\frac{1}{3}$

ANSWER KEY *(cont.)*

Week 12: Day 4 (page 71)

1. $\frac{3}{8}$; $3 \div 8$

2. Possible answer: I think writing a division expression is better because it takes less time than drawing a model.

Week 12: Day 5 (page 72)

1. Possible fraction model:

2. Possible fraction model:

3. Campers seated at tables with 10 chairs will get the most pizza. They receive $\frac{8}{10}$ or $\frac{4}{5}$ of a pizza. Campers seated at tables with 8 chairs receive only $\frac{6}{8}$ or $\frac{3}{4}$ of a pizza. $\frac{8}{10}$ is greater than $\frac{6}{8}$.

Week 13: Day 1 (page 73)

1. The area will be less than 3 square feet because 3 is being multiplied by a factor less than 1.

2. $\frac{3}{4} + \frac{3}{4} + \frac{3}{4}$

3. $3 \times \frac{3}{4}$

Week 13: Day 2 (page 74)

1. $\frac{9}{4}$ or $2\frac{1}{4}$ square feet; multiply; $3 \times \frac{3}{4} = \frac{9}{4}$ or $2\frac{1}{4}$

2. $\frac{4}{3}$ or $1\frac{1}{3}$ square feet; multiply; $2 \times \frac{2}{3} = \frac{4}{3}$ or $1\frac{1}{3}$

Week 13: Day 3 (page 75)

$\frac{5}{6} + \frac{5}{6} + \frac{5}{6} + \frac{5}{6} + \frac{5}{6} + \frac{5}{6} + \frac{5}{6} + \frac{5}{6} = \frac{40}{6}$ or $6\frac{4}{6}$ or $6\frac{2}{3}$;
$8 \times \frac{5}{6} = \frac{40}{6}$ or $6\frac{4}{6}$ or $6\frac{2}{3}$

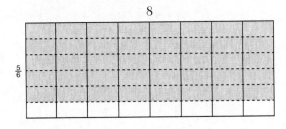

Week 13: Day 4 (page 76)

1. $\frac{21}{4}$ or $5\frac{1}{4}$ miles; Possible strategies: repeated addition, multiplication, fraction model;
$\frac{3}{4} + \frac{3}{4} + \frac{3}{4} + \frac{3}{4} + \frac{3}{4} + \frac{3}{4} + \frac{3}{4} = \frac{21}{4}$ or $5\frac{1}{4}$; $7 \times \frac{3}{4} = \frac{21}{4}$ or $5\frac{1}{4}$

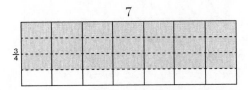

2. Possible answer: I think using repeated addition is easier because I can add the numerators and then simplify the fraction.

Week 13: Day 5 (page 77)

1. $\frac{2}{5} \times 60 = \frac{120}{5} = 24$ times

2. $\frac{1}{3} \times 60 = \frac{60}{3} = 20$ times

3. Possible answers: $24 + 20 = 44$, $60 - 44 = 16$ times; $\frac{2}{5} + \frac{1}{3} = \frac{6}{15} + \frac{5}{15} = \frac{11}{15}$, $\frac{15}{15} - \frac{11}{15} = \frac{4}{15}$, $\frac{4}{15} \times 60 = \frac{240}{15} = 16$ times

Week 14: Day 1 (page 78)

1. $\frac{3}{5}$ of the shoes are athletic shoes. $\frac{1}{4}$ of the athletic shoes are blue.

2. Multiply the fractions to solve the problem.

3. The product will be less than $\frac{3}{5}$ because $\frac{3}{5}$ is being multiplied by a factor less than 1.

Week 14: Day 2 (page 79)

1. $\frac{3}{20}$; multiply the fractions; $\frac{1}{4} \times \frac{3}{5} = \frac{3}{20}$

2. $\frac{10}{24}$ or $\frac{5}{12}$; multiply the fractions;
$\frac{2}{3} \times \frac{5}{8} = \frac{10}{24}$ or $\frac{5}{12}$

Week 14: Day 3 (page 80)

$\frac{3}{8}$

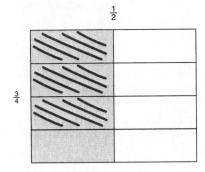

ANSWER KEY *(cont.)*

Week 14: Day 4 (page 81)

1. $\frac{5}{12}$ of a tub; Possible strategies: fraction model, equations, number line; $\frac{1}{2} \times \frac{5}{6} = \frac{5}{12}$

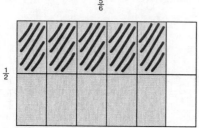

2. Possible answer: I think drawing a fraction model is easier because it helps me visualize the problem.

Week 14: Day 5 (page 82)

1.

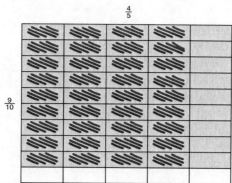

2. The area of the window is $\frac{9}{10} \times \frac{4}{5} = \frac{36}{50}$ square meter. Reanna will get paid $72. $(100 \times \frac{36}{50} = \frac{3600}{50} = 72)$

Week 15: Day 1 (page 83)

1. The fifth grade bulletin board will be less than 3 square meters because it is being multiplied by $\frac{7}{10}$, which is a factor less than 1.

2. The sixth grade bulletin board will be greater than 3 square meters because it is being multiplied by $\frac{12}{10}$, which is a factor greater than 1.

Week 15: Day 2 (page 84)

1. Sixth-grade bulletin board has a greater area; draw a model and compare factors; $\frac{12}{10}$ is greater than $\frac{7}{10}$

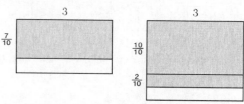

2. Seventh- and eighth-grade science display areas are the same; draw a model and compare the products; $\frac{1}{2} \times \frac{1}{3} = \frac{1}{6}$ and $\frac{1}{3} \times \frac{1}{2} = \frac{1}{6}$

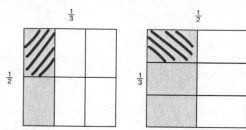

Week 15: Day 3 (page 85)

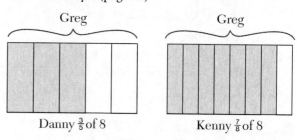

Kenny received a higher score because $\frac{7}{8}$ of 8 is greater than $\frac{3}{5}$ of 8.

Week 15: Day 4 (page 86)

1. Answers will vary, but the problem with a product less than $3\frac{1}{3}$ should be multiplied by a factor less than 1; Possible answer: $3\frac{1}{3} \times \frac{7}{10} = \frac{10}{3} \times \frac{7}{10} = \frac{70}{30} = 2\frac{10}{30}$ or $2\frac{1}{3}$; $2\frac{1}{3} < 3\frac{1}{3}$; the problem with a product greater than $3\frac{1}{3}$ should be multiplied by a factor greater than 1; Possible answer: $3\frac{1}{3} \times \frac{9}{8} = \frac{10}{3} \times \frac{9}{8} = \frac{90}{24} = 3\frac{18}{24}$ or $3\frac{3}{4}$; $3\frac{3}{4} > 3\frac{1}{3}$

2. Possible answer: To find a product less than $3\frac{1}{3}$, I multiplied by a factor less than 1. To find a greater product than $3\frac{1}{3}$, I multiplied by a factor greater than 1.

ANSWER KEY *(cont.)*

Week 15: Day 5 (page 87)

1. 8 daisies; $\frac{4}{3} \times 6 = \frac{24}{3} = 8$
2. 4 carnations; $\frac{2}{3} \times 6 = \frac{12}{3} = 4$

Week 16: Day 1 (page 88)

1. Yes, her calculations are correct so far.
2. $\frac{15}{5} = 3$
3. Sydney needs to add $\frac{15}{5}$ and $\frac{3}{10}$.

Week 16: Day 2 (page 89)

1. $3\frac{3}{10}$ of the boxes are chocolate chip; multiply the fractions $\frac{3}{5} \times 5\frac{1}{2} = \frac{3}{5} \times \frac{11}{1} = \frac{33}{10} = 3\frac{3}{10}$
2. $\frac{51}{80}$ quarts of milk; multiply the fractions; $\frac{3}{8} \times 1\frac{7}{10} = \frac{3}{8} \times \frac{17}{10} = \frac{51}{80}$

Week 16: Day 3 (page 90)

$7\frac{11}{12} \frac{5}{1}$; $6 + \frac{3}{2} + \frac{2}{6} + \frac{1}{12} = 6 + \frac{18}{12} + \frac{4}{12} + \frac{1}{12} = 6\frac{23}{12}$ $= 7\frac{11}{24}$

	2	$\frac{1}{2}$
3	6	$\frac{3}{2}$
$\frac{1}{6}$	$\frac{2}{6}$	$\frac{1}{12}$

Week 16: Day 4 (page 91)

1. $\frac{21}{16}$ or $1\frac{5}{16}$ square feet; Possible strategies: fraction model; equations; number line; $\frac{3}{4} + \frac{9}{16} = \frac{12}{16} + \frac{9}{16} = \frac{21}{16} = 1\frac{5}{16}$

	1	$\frac{3}{4}$
$\frac{3}{4}$	$\frac{3}{4}$	$\frac{9}{16}$

2. Possible answer: I think drawing a fraction model is better because it makes multiplying the factors easier.

Week 16: Day 5 (page 92)

1. $7\frac{1}{2}$ cups of raisins; $3 \times 2\frac{1}{2} = 3 \times \frac{5}{2} = \frac{15}{2} = 7\frac{1}{2}$
2. 2 cups of raisins; $\frac{4}{5} \times 2\frac{1}{2} = \frac{4}{5} \times \frac{5}{2} = \frac{21}{10} = 2$
3. $3\frac{3}{4}$ cups of raisins; $1\frac{1}{2} \times 2\frac{1}{2} = \frac{3}{2} \times \frac{5}{2} = \frac{15}{4} = 3\frac{3}{4}$
4. Rick has the most raisins in his recipe. Possible explanation: I know Rick has the most raisins because he triples the amount of Greta's raisins and 3 is a greater factor than $\frac{4}{5}$ and $1\frac{1}{2}$.

Week 17: Day 1 (page 93)

1. B and C
2. Yes, the order matters in a division equation. Five is being divided by $\frac{1}{4}$ in the equation.

Week 17: Day 2 (page 94)

1. $5 \div \frac{1}{4} = 5 \times \frac{4}{1} = 20$
2. $2 \div \frac{1}{6} = 2 \times \frac{1}{6} = 12$

Week 17: Day 3 (page 95)

$6 \div \frac{1}{2} = 12$ flyers

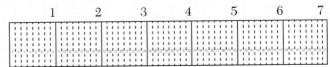

Week 17: Day 4 (page 96)

1. 56 servings; Strategies: bar model; equation; $7 \div \frac{1}{8} = 56$

1	2	3	4	5	6	7

2. Possible answer: I like drawing a bar model because it helps me visualize how many $\frac{1}{8}$ cup servings are in 7 cups.

Week 17: Day 5 (page 97)

1. Pictures will vary, but should show how many one-third cups are in each ingredient.
2. $9 \div \frac{1}{3} = 27$ one-third cups rice cereal; $2 \div \frac{1}{3} = 6$ one-third cups chocolate chips; $1 \div \frac{1}{3} = 3$ one-third cups peanut butter
3. 36 one-third cups ingredients; Possible explanation: I found the total number of one-third cups ingredients by adding all of the one-third cups of rice cereal, chocolate chips, and peanut butter.

Week 18: Day 1 (page 98)

1. The solution will be less than $\frac{1}{2}$ because Marcus is sharing $\frac{1}{2}$ of a bottle among 10 drinks.
2. $\frac{1}{2} \div 10$

Week 18: Day 2 (page 99)

1. $\frac{1}{20}$ of the bottle; divide; $\frac{1}{2} \div 10 = \frac{1}{2} \times \frac{1}{10} = \frac{1}{20}$
2. $\frac{1}{15}$ of the bottle; divide; $\frac{1}{3} \div 5 = \frac{1}{3} \times \frac{1}{5} = \frac{1}{15}$

ANSWER KEY *(cont.)*

Week 18: Day 3 (page 100)

$\frac{1}{8} \div 4 = \frac{1}{32}$ of the pan

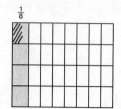

Week 18: Day 4 (page 101)

1. $\frac{1}{10}$ of the box; Possible strategies: fraction model, equations, number line;
$\frac{1}{5} \div 2 = \frac{1}{10}$

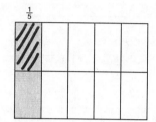

2. Possible answer: I like drawing a fraction model better because it helps me visualize how to divide a fraction by a whole number.

Week 18: Day 5 (page 102)

1. Pictures will vary, but should show how much of each ingredient Patty will need to make 6 identical sundaes.

2. $\frac{1}{2} \div 6 = \frac{1}{12}$ gallon ice cream; $\frac{1}{4} \div 6 = \frac{1}{24}$ pound chocolate chunks; $\frac{1}{3} \div 6 = \frac{1}{18}$ cup marshmallows; $\frac{1}{5} \div 6 = \frac{1}{30}$ jar cherries

3. Each sundae would have less of each ingredient because she is dividing the ingredients by a greater number of sundaes.

Week 19: Day 1 (page 103)

1. There are $2\frac{1}{2}$- cup servings in 1 cup of macaroni. There are 8 total cups of macaroni. The solution must be greater than 8 cups of macaroni.

2. Possible answer: How many servings of macaroni can she make?

Week 19: Day 2 (page 104)

1. 16 servings; divide 8 by $\frac{1}{2}$; $8 \div \frac{1}{2} = 16$
2. $\frac{1}{8}$ of the whole cake; divide $\frac{1}{2}$ by 4; $\frac{1}{2} \div 4 = \frac{1}{8}$

Week 19: Day 3 (page 105)

Story problem	Model	Equation
Story problems will vary, but should show $\frac{1}{3}$ being divided by 4.		$\frac{1}{3} \div 4 = \frac{1}{12}$

Week 19: Day 4 (page 106)

1. 8 dogs; Possible strategies: fraction model, equations; $2 \div \frac{1}{4} = 8$

2. Possible answer: I think drawing a number line is better because it shows how many $\frac{1}{4}$ cups are in 2 cups of shampoo.

Week 19: Day 5 (page 107)

1. Pictures will vary, but should show how much of each whole ingredient is in each serving of salsa.

2. $\frac{1}{2} \div 12 = \frac{1}{24}$ cup cilantro; $\frac{4}{2} \div 12 = \frac{1}{48}$ cup onion; $\frac{1}{3} \div 12 = \frac{1}{36}$ cup lime juice; $\frac{1}{6} \div 12 = \frac{1}{72}$ cup garlic

3. Each serving would have more of each ingredient because she is dividing the ingredients by a smaller number of servings.

Week 20: Day 1 (page 108)

1. The sandwich is 5 feet long. There are 6 people sharing the sandwich equally.

2. Each person will get less than 1 foot of the sandwich because there are more people (6) than feet of sandwich available (5).

3. 60 inches in 5 feet; 1 foot = 12 inches; $5 \times 12 = 60$

Week 20: Day 2 (page 109)

1. 10 inches per person; change 5 feet to inches and divide by 6; $5 \times 12 = 60$ inches; $60 \div 6 = 10$

2. 15 inches per guest; change 5 feet to inches and divide by 4; $5 \times 12 = 60$ inches; $60 \div 4 = 15$

#51617—*180 Days of Problem Solving*

ANSWER KEY *(cont.)*

Week 20: Day 3 (page 110)

$\frac{1}{6}$ of 12 = $\frac{1}{6} \times \frac{12}{1} = \frac{12}{6} = 2$; $\frac{1}{3}$ of 12 = $\frac{1}{3} \times \frac{12}{1} = \frac{12}{3} = 4$;

$\frac{1}{2}$ of 12 = $\frac{1}{2} \times \frac{12}{1} = \frac{12}{2} = 6$; $\frac{2}{3}$ of 12 = $\frac{2}{3} \times \frac{12}{1} = \frac{24}{3} = 8$

Feet	Inches
0	0
$\frac{1}{6}$	2
$\frac{1}{4} = \frac{1}{4}$	4
$\frac{1}{4} = \frac{1}{4}$	6
$\frac{1}{4} = \frac{1}{4}$	8

Week 20: Day 4 (page 111)

1. 2 hours and 24 minutes; Possible strategies: use a clock, number line, change 24 hours into minutes and divide by 10, change 24 hours to minutes and subtract groups of 60; 24 hours = 1,440 minutes (24 × 60 = 1,440); 1,440 ÷ 10 = 144 minutes; 144 − 60 = 84; 84 − 60 = 24; 2 hours and 24 minutes

2. Possible answer: I think changing 24 hours to minutes, dividing by 10, and subtracting groups of 60 is easier because it tells me how many hours and minutes each nurse will spend at the hospital.

Week 20: Day 5 (page 112)

1. $2\frac{3}{6}$ or $2\frac{1}{2}$ miles; 15 ÷ 6 = $\frac{12}{6}$ = $2\frac{3}{6}$ or $2\frac{1}{2}$

2. $2\frac{1}{2}$ miles = 2 miles and 2,640 feet ($\frac{1}{2} \times$ 5,280 feet = 2,640 feet)

3. $2\frac{1}{2}$ miles = 13,200 feet (2 miles = 5,280 × 2 = 10,560; $\frac{1}{2}$ mile = $\frac{1}{2} \times$ 5,280 feet = 2,640 feet 10,560 + 2,640 = 13,200 feet)

Week 21: Day 1 (page 113)

1. Possible answer: Bottles of Perfume

2. Count the number of Xs on the line plot. Each X represents one bottle of perfume. There are 12 bottles.

3. Ounces

Week 21: Day 2 (page 114)

1. 12 bottles; count the number of Xs on the line plot; 12 Xs

2. 7 ounces; add the number of ounces for all of the bottles; $(3 \times \frac{1}{4}) + (5 \times \frac{1}{2}) + \frac{3}{4} + (3 \times 1)$ $= \frac{3}{4} + 2\frac{1}{2} + \frac{3}{4} + 3 = 7$

Week 21: Day 3 (page 115)

Titles and labels may vary, but should include the correct number of Xs for each bottle.

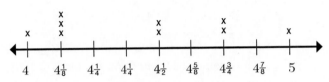

Bakery Spice Rack Inventory

Sizes of bottles (ounces)

Week 21: Day 4 (page 116)

1. $19\frac{7}{8}$ inches; Possible strategies: fraction bars; number line; equations; $2\frac{1}{8} + (2 \times 2\frac{2}{8}) + (2 \times 2\frac{4}{8}) + (3 \times 2\frac{6}{8}) = 19\frac{7}{8}$

2. Possible answer: I think using equations is better because I can use repeated addition for the fractions that repeat on the line plot, then I can add all of the fractions together.

Week 21: Day 5 (page 117)

1. Titles and labels may vary, but should include the correct number of Xs for the number of bags of birdseed.

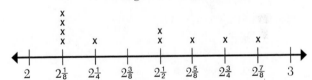

Bags of Birdseed

Weight (pounds)

2. $2\frac{4}{10}$ or $2\frac{2}{5}$ pounds per bag; total of 24 pounds of birdseed $(4 \times 2\frac{1}{8}) + 2\frac{1}{4} + (2 \times 2\frac{1}{2}) + 2\frac{5}{8} + 2\frac{3}{4} + 2\frac{7}{8}$ $= 24$; $\frac{24}{10} = 2\frac{4}{10}$ or $2\frac{2}{5}$

Week 22: Day 1 (page 118)

1. 2 tens or 20

2. 2 ones or 2

3. Possible answer: Understanding place value helps me know how much each digit is worth in a number.

ANSWER KEY *(cont.)*

Week 22: Day 2 (page 119)

1. Yes, the value of the digit 2 in 325 is 10 times greater than the value of the digit 2 in 682; find the value of the digit 2 in each number; 20 is 10 times greater than 2

2. No, the value of the digit 5 in 539 is 10 times greater than the value of the digit 5 in 254, not $\frac{1}{10}$ times greater; find the value of the digit 5 in each number; 500 is 10 times greater than 50

Week 22: Day 3 (page 120)

1. The shading shows 1 out of 100 equal parts. Fraction: $\frac{1}{100}$; Decimal: 0.01

2. 10 times greater; Possible explanation: The digit 1 in 0.1 is 10 times greater than the digit 1 in 0.01 because 0.1 is equal to $\frac{1}{10}$ or $\frac{10}{100}$ and 0.01 is equal to $\frac{1}{100}$.

Week 22: Day 4 (page 121)

1. Statement 1 is incorrect. The 8 on the left is 10 times the value of the 8 on the right, not 100 times. Statement 2 is correct. The 8 on the right is $\frac{1}{10}$ the value of the 8 on the left.

2. Possible answer: Understanding place value helps me know how many times greater a digit is than another digit in a number.

Week 22: Day 5 (page 122)

1. Models will vary, but should show that the digit 1 in 1.8 is 100 times greater than the digit 1 in 0.018.

2. Models will vary, but should show that the digit 8 in 1.8 is 100 times greater than the digit 8 in 0.018.

3. 100 times wider; $0.018 \times 100 = 1.8$

Week 23: Day 1 (page 123)

1. Possible answers: $3.8 \times 10 \times 10 \times 10$ and $3.8 \times 1,000$

2. The exponent 3 indicates how many times to multiply 3.8 by 10. The number becomes 10 times greater each time it is multiplied.

Week 23: Day 2 (page 124)

1. $3.8 \times 10^3 = 3,800$; Write the base number, look at the exponent to know how many spaces to the right to move the decimal point, and fill in zeros in the empty place values.

2. $950 \div 10^3 = 0.95$; Write the base number, look at the exponent to know how many spaces to the left to move the decimal point, and fill in zeros if needed.

Week 23: Day 3 (page 125)

1.

Number	× 10¹	× 10²	× 10³
61.5	615	6,150	61,500
0.01	0.1	1	10

2.

Number	÷ 10¹	÷ 10²	÷ 10³
31.3	3.13	0.313	0.0313
663.4	66.34	6.634	0.6634

3. When multiplying by powers of 10, the number gets 10 times greater each time. It shifts the digits of the decimal to the right. When dividing by powers of 10, the number gets 10 times less each time. It shifts the digits of the decimal to the left.

Week 23: Day 4 (page 126)

1. $4.752 \times 100 = 475.2$; $4.752 \div 10 = 0.4752$

2. Possible answer: I used guess and check, but I also know that multiplying makes a greater answer and division makes a lesser answer.

Week 23: Day 5 (page 127)

1.

Less than 0.8	Equal to 0.8	Greater than 0.8
$80 \div 10^3$	$800 \div 10^3$	8×10^1
$0.8 \div 10^1$		0.8×10^1
0.008×10^1		$80 \div 10^1$
		0.8×10^2
		0.08×10^2
		0.08×10^3
		0.008×10^3
		$800 \div 10^2$

2. Possible answer: I know that when a base number is being multiplied by a power of ten, the decimal point moves to the right the same number of spaces as the exponent. When the base number is divided by a power of ten, the decimal moves to the left the same number of spaces as the exponent.

Week 24: Day 1 (page 128)

1. fifty-seven hundredths
2. $\frac{57}{100}$
3. 5
4. 7

ANSWER KEY *(cont.)*

Week 24: Day 2 (page 129)

1. Possible answers: 0.50 + 0.07; 5 tenths + 7 hundredths; $(5 \times \frac{1}{10}) + (7 \times \frac{1}{100})$

2. Possible answers: $3\frac{196}{1000}$; 3 + 0.1 + 0.09 + 0.006; 3 ones + 1 tenth + 9 hundredths + 6 thousandths; $3 + \frac{108}{1000} + \frac{90}{1000} + \frac{6}{1000}$; $(3 \times 1) + (1 \times \frac{1}{10}) + (9 \times \frac{1}{100}) + (6 \times \frac{1}{1000})$

Week 24: Day 3 (page 130)

Standard form	Word form	Fraction form	Expanded form
2.6	two and six tenths	$2\frac{6}{10}$	$(2 \times 1) + (6 \times \frac{1}{10})$
3.64	three and sixty-four hundredths	$3\frac{64}{100}$	$(3 \times 1) + (6 \times \frac{1}{10}) + (4 \times \frac{1}{100})$
2.086	two and eighty-six thousandths	$2\frac{86}{1000}$	$(2 \times 1) + (0 \times \frac{1}{10}) + (8 \times \frac{1}{100}) + (6 \times \frac{1}{1000})$

Week 24: Day 4 (page 131)

1.
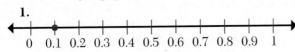

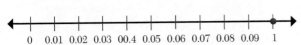

2. The similarities are that both number lines use decimals and both start with zero. The differences are that the first number line counts by $\frac{1}{10}$ and ends with 1, while the second number line counts by $\frac{1}{100}$ and ends with 0.10.

Week 24: Day 5 (page 132)

1. Sapphire: 0.326 grams; Garnet: 0.346 grams; Amethyst: 0.238 grams; Emerald: 0.18 grams; Topaz: 0.692 grams; Diamond: 0.032 grams

Week 25: Day 1 (page 133)

1. 1 one; 1 one
2. 5 tenths, 5 tenths
3. 0 hundredths; 7 hundredths
4. $1\frac{508}{1000}$ and $1\frac{570}{1000}$

Week 25: Day 2 (page 134)

1. 1.57 MB; compare the numbers; 1.57 > 1.508

2. 0.009 MB; compare the numbers; 0.009 < 0.09

Week 25: Day 3 (page 135)

1. 0.91 is closer to 1

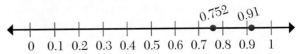

2. 0.01 is closer to 0.

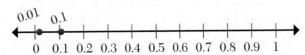

Week 25: Day 4 (page 136)

1. Answers should be between 3.140 and 3.150; Possible answers: 3.141; 3.145; 3.149; Possible strategies: number line, list, base-10 models; write decimals as fractions

2. Possible answer: I think using a number line is better because it helps me order numbers from least to greatest.

Week 25: Day 5 (page 137)

1. 19.073, 19.7, 19.73, 19.743, 19.751, 19.82, 19.9, 20.1; students should have made a circle around the first four numbers and a circle around the last four numbers

2. The vertical jump 19.751 is the closest to 19.75 because it is only 1 thousandth away.

Week 26: Day 1 (page 138)

1.
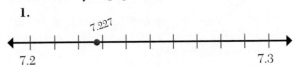

2. 7.2; 7.227 is closer to 7.2 than 7.3 on the number line

Week 26: Day 2 (page 139)

1. 7.2; use a number line; 7.227 is closer to 7.2 than 7.3 on a number line

2. 8.7; use a number line; 8.695 is closer 8.7 than 8.6 on a number line

Week 26: Day 3 (page 140)

Point B is between 0.03 and 0.04. Rounded to the nearest hundredth, Point B is 0.04. Rounded to the nearest tenth, Point B is 0.

ANSWER KEY (cont.)

Week 26: Day 4 (page 141)

1. Answers should be between 11.15 and 11.24; Possible answers: 11.16; 11.19; 11.23; Possible strategies: number line, list, base-10 models; write decimals as fractions

2. Possible answer: I like using a number line because it helps me round numbers to the nearest tenth or hundredth more easily.

Week 26: Day 5 (page 142)

1. Starting decimals will vary, but should round to the given decimals.

Starting decimal	Decimal rounded to the nearest tenth	Decimal rounded to the nearest hundredth
0.431	0.4	0.43
3.582	3.6	3.58
9.911	9.9	9.91
6.224	6.2	6.22
0.092	0.1	0.09

2. Yes, there can be more than one possible starting decimal as long as the number rounds to the nearest tenth and nearest hundredth shown in the table.

Week 27: Day 1 (page 143)

1. The sum will be greater than 24 because adding the whole numbers give 24 ounces and adding the decimals will make it greater than 24.

2. The sum will be less than 25 because both addends are less than 12.5, so the decimals will be less than 1 whole.

Week 27: Day 2 (page 144)

1. 24.69 ounces; add the decimals; 12.26 + 12.43 = 24.69

2. 13.76 ounces; add 8 and the decimals; 8 + 4.4 + 1.36 = 13.76

Week 27: Day 3 (page 145)

1. 2.23

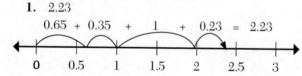

0.65 + 0.35 + 1 + 0.23 = 2.23

Week 27: Day 4 (page 146)

1. Hamburger ($4.75), water ($2.75), popcorn ($1.75), and licorice ($0.75); exactly $10.00; Possible strategies: guess and check, number line, equations; use estimation; add the amounts and then subtract the item that makes the amount over $10.00; $2.75 + $3.00 + $4.75 + $1.75 + $0.75 = $13.00; $13.00 – $10.00 = $3.00; $13.00 – $3.00 (hot dog) = $10.00

2. Possible answer: I prefer using estimation and equations because I can add the amounts together and then subtract the item(s) that make the amount over $10.00.

Week 27: Day 5 (page 147)

1. 150 points

2. Possible answer: First, I added all of the decimals together. Then, I added the number of points he had left on the card. I found that the total points he started with were 150 points.

Week 28: Day 1 (page 148)

1. No, Quinn's answer is not reasonable. Using estimation, 52 – 6 or 53 – 7 is 46, so the answer should be around 46 pounds. Quinn's answer is too high.

2. Quinn did not write the numbers in the correct place value by lining up the decimal points.

Week 28: Day 2 (page 149)

1. 46.25 pounds; subtract; 52.75 – 6.5 = 46.25

2. 0.52 ounces; subtract; 1.4 – 0.88 = 0.52

Week 28: Day 3 (page 150)

2.8

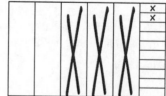

Week 28: Day 4 (page 151)

1. 1.89 ounces of chocolate pretzels; Possible strategies: number line, equations; bar model; 5.76 + 3.2 + 5.15 = 14.11; 16 – 14.11 = 1.89

2. Possible answer: I think using equations is better because I can add the amounts together and then subtract the total from 16.

ANSWER KEY *(cont.)*

Week 28: Day 5 (page 152)

1. $96.24; $42.17 + $23.90 + $11.93 + $18.24 = $96.24
2. $3.76 left; $100.00 – $96.24 = $3.76

Week 29: Day 1 (page 153)

1. A reasonable estimate would be less than $5.00 because Wade is buying 5 pens, and each costs less than $1.00.
2. Wade's estimate was less than $5.00, so his solution of $36.50 is unreasonable.
3. Wade uses five hundredths grids and shades $\frac{73}{100}$ on each. This makes 5 groups of 0.73. From there, he can count tenths and hundredths and add them up to get the correct solution.

Week 29: Day 2 (page 154)

1. $3.65; estimate the cost and then compare the solution to estimate; estimate should be less than $5.00; $3.65 is less than $5.00, so solution is reasonable; 5 × $0.73 = $3.65
2. $9.57; estimate the cost and then compare the solution to estimate; estimate should be about $9.00; $9.57 is about $9.00, so solution is reasonable; 3 × $3.19 = $9.57

Week 29: Day 3 (page 155)

1 group of 1 = 1; 1 group of 0.4 = 0.4; 1 group of 0.4 = 0.4; 4 groups of 0.04 = 0.16; Total area: 1.96 square centimeters

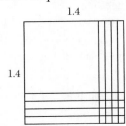

Week 29: Day 4 (page 156)

1. 4.3 × 7.5 = 32.25; Possible strategies: guess and check; area model; equations; estimation
2. Possible answer: I like using estimation because I know that the product is about 32, which helped me know that the factors should be about 4 and 7.

Week 29: Day 5 (page 157)

1. $3.25 + ($2.25 × 12.6) + (3.5 × $0.30)
2. $32.65

Week 30: Day 1 (page 158)

1. Chloe's estimate is greater than the actual price because $4.00 × 2.5 is $10.00, which is greater than $8.85.
2. Chloe's brother's estimate is less than the actual price because $3.00 × 2.5 is $7.50, which is less than $8.85.

Week 30: Day 2 (page 159)

1. $3.54; estimate the cost and then compare the solution to estimate; estimate should be greater than $3.00; $3.54 is greater than $3.00, so solution is reasonable; $8.85 ÷ 2.5 = $3.54
2. 0.25 pounds; estimate the weight and then compare the solution to estimate; estimate should be less than 0.5 pound; 0.25 is less than 0.5, so solution is reasonable; 2.5 ÷ 10 = 0.25

Week 30: Day 3 (page 160)

There are 4 groups of 0.2 in 0.8; 0.8 ÷ 0.2 = 4 pieces

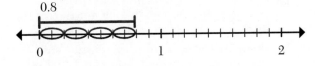

Week 30: Day 4 (page 161)

1. 5 ÷ 0.01 = 500; Possible strategies: guess and check; area model; equations; estimation; multiplication; 500 × 0.01 = 500 × $\frac{1}{100}$ = $\frac{500}{100}$ or 5.
2. Possible answer: I prefer using multiplication because I can multiply a number times 500 to get 5. I can find how many hundredths are in 5 wholes.

Week 30: Day 5 (page 162)

1. $5.50; add the amounts together; $4.65 + $0.85 = $5.50
2. 7 times; $38.50 ÷ ($4.65 + $0.85) = $38.50 ÷ $5.50 = 7

Week 31: Day 1 (page 163)

1. Possible question: Is the gecko longer than the salamander?
2. 1 cm = 10 mm; 1 mm = 0.1 cm; 36 cm = 360 mm; 89 mm = 8.9 cm

ANSWER KEY (cont.)

Week 31: Day 2 (page 164)

1. The gecko is longer by 271 mm or 27.1 cm; convert the units to the same unit, compare them, and then subtract; 360 mm > 89 mm; 360 − 89 = 271; 36 cm > 8.9 cm; 36 − 8.9 = 27.1

2. The elephant drinks more by 65,000 mL or 65 L; convert the units to the same unit, compare them, and then subtract; 200,000 mL > 135,000 mL; 200,000 − 135,000 = 65,000 mL; 200 L > 135 L; 200 − 135 = 65 L

Week 31: Day 3 (page 165)

The emperor penguin weighs more by 17,630 g or 17.63 kg.

Penguin	Grams (g)	Kilograms (kg)
emperor penguin	23,130	23.13
macaroni penguin	5,500	5.5

Week 31: Day 4 (page 166)

1. The length of the airplane is longer than its wingspan by 610 cm or 6.1 m; Possible strategies: convert units to centimeters; convert units to meters; compare the units; subtract

2. Possible answer: I think converting the units to centimeters is easier because I'm better at comparing and subtracting whole numbers than decimals.

Week 31: Day 5 (page 167)

1. 770,00 grams or 770 kilograms per week; 55,000 × 2 = 110,000 grams per day; 110,000 × 7 = 770,000 grams per week; 55 × 2 = 110 kilograms per day; 110 × 7 = 770 kilograms per week

2. No, bundle of hay is 680,000 grams or 680 kilograms. They need 770,000 grams or 770 kilograms per week.

Week 32: Day 1 (page 168)

1. Mrs. Moore will not consider a rectangle because all 4 sides are not equal.

2. Mrs. Moore will not consider a parallelogram because all 4 sides are not equal.

3. Although all of the sides of an equilateral triangle are equal, the triangle only has 3 sides, so Mrs. Moore will not consider picking it.

Week 32: Day 2 (page 169)

1. Rhombus and square; All four sides are equal.

2. Rectangle and square; All four angles are equal.

Week 32: Day 3 (page 170)

1.

Example	Non-example
All 4 sides are equal	All four sides are not equal
Opposite sides are equal	No sides are equal
Opposite angles are equal	No angles are equal

2. Statements will vary, but should include two shapes with examples and non-examples; Possible example: Sometimes a parallelogram is a rectangle.

Week 32: Day 4 (page 171)

1. Possible shapes: To make a trapezoid, one vertex needs to be moved. Now, there is one pair of parallel sides instead of two. To make a parallelogram, no changes are necessary. The square already has two pairs of equal sides and parallel sides.

2. Possible answer: It was easier to make a parallelogram because a square is a parallelogram. Both shapes have two pairs of equal sides that are parallel.

Week 32: Day 5 (page 172)

1. Pictures will vary, but each shape should have 4 sides with adjacent sides equal in length. Possible kites: rhombus, square

2. Kites have 4 sides with adjacent sides that are equal in length.

3. Kite B is different from the other quadrilaterals because it has an angle greater than 180 degrees (straight angle) and is concave.

Week 33: Day 1 (page 173)

1. square and rhombus

2. square and rectangle

3. square

Week 33: Day 2 (page 174)

1. square; all of the sides and all of the angles are equal; compare attributes of quadrilaterals

2. equilateral triangle; all of the sides and all of the angles are equal; compare attributes of triangles

Week 33: Day 3 (page 175)

Title: Quadrilaterals; Parallelograms: square, rectangle, rhombus; Non-parallelograms: trapezoid, kite

ANSWER KEY *(cont.)*

Week 33: Day 4 (page 176)

1.

 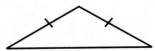

obtuse scalene triangle   obtuse isosceles triangle

2. Possible answer: It is impossible to draw an obtuse equilateral triangle because if all of the sides are equal in a triangle, all of the angles must also be equal. It is impossible to have 3 obtuse angles in a triangle because the angles will be more than 180 degrees.

Week 33: Day 5 (page 177)

1. Possible examples: 5-point quadrilateral is a square; 4-point quadrilateral is a rhombus; 3-point quadrilateral is a rectangle; 2-point quadrilateral is a parallelogram; 1-point shape is a kite.

2. 5-point quadrilateral: all sides equal, all angles equal, two pairs of parallel lines, opposite sides equal, adjacent sides equal; 4-point quadrilateral: all sides equal, two pairs of parallel lines, opposite sides equal, adjacent sides equal; 3-point quadrilateral: all angles equal, two pairs of parallel lines, opposite sides equal; 2-point quadrilateral: two pairs of parallel lines, opposite sides equal; 1-point shape: adjacent sides equal

3. A 0-point quadrilateral is possible. An example is a trapezoid as it does not have any of the listed properties.

Week 34: Day 1 (page 178)

1. 3 pages per day
2. 6 pages per day
3. Jack's number of pages is two times Abby's number of pages. Possible explanation: I see on the chart that Jack read twice as many pages as Abby each day.

Week 34: Day 2 (page 179)

1. Abby: 12 pages; Jack: 24 pages; Complete the table and look for patterns to find the total number of pages both Abby and Jack read after 4 days.

Day	Abby's pages read	Jack's pages read
0	0	0
1	3	6
2	6	12
3	9	18
4	12	24

2. Henry: 20 pages; Jane: 40 pages; Complete the table and look for patterns to find the total number of pages both Henry and Jane read after 4 days.

Day	Henry's pages read	Jane's pages read
0	0	0
1	5	10
2	10	20
3	15	30
4	20	40

Week 34: Day 3 (page 180)

Day	Food pellets eaten by Gordon's turtle	Food pellets eaten by Lexie's turtle
0	0	0
1	4	8
2	8	16
3	12	24
4	16	32
5	20	40
6	24	48
7	28	56

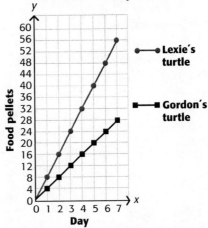

Food Pellets Eaten by Turtles

ANSWER KEY *(cont.)*

Week 34: Day 4 (page 181)

1. Clay's table:

Day	Clay's total number of levels cleared	Cameron's total number of levels cleared
0	0	0
1	3	9
2	6	18
3	9	27
4	12	36
5	15	45
6	18	54
7	21	63

2. Cameron's graph:

Video Game Levels Passed

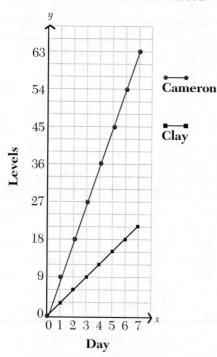

Possible answer: I prefer to present data in a graph because it helps me see if the data is increasing or decreasing. Also, it helps me to compare two sets of data.

Week 34: Day 5 (page 182)

Coaster rides	Passengers on Kids Minifun Coaster	Passengers on Giant Racer Coaster
0	0	0
1	10	20
2	20	40
3	30	60
4	40	80
5	50	100
6	60	120
7	70	140
8	80	160
9	90	180
10	100	200

Passengers Carried

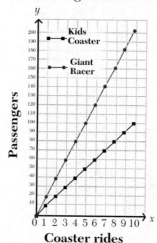

1. Kids Minifun Coaster: 100; Giant Racer Coaster: 200

2. After the 20 rides, there will be 200 passengers on the Kids Coaster and 400 passengers on the Giant Racer. After 60 rides, there will be 600 passengers on the Kids Coaster and 1,200 passengers on the Giant Racer.

3. Kids Minifun Coaster: 10; Giant Racer Coaster: 20; Possible Explanation: The Kids Minifun Coaster is increasing by 10 and the Giant Racer is increasing by 20.

ANSWER KEY *(cont.)*

Week 35: Day 1 (page 183)

1. Possible answer: I predict the shape will have four sides (quadrilateral). Since there are four points given, the shape will have four vertices and four sides.

2.

x	y
2	1
4	1
6	4
0	4

3. Yes, the order matters. Possible explanation: The x-coordinate must be listed first because it is located along the horizontal x-axis. The y-coordinate must be listed second because it is located along the vertical y-axis.

Week 35: Day 2 (page 184)

1. Trapezoid; plot and connect the points; use attributes of shapes to determine what shape is formed

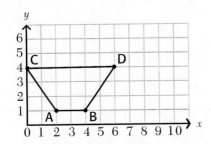

2. Triangle (scalene, right); plot and connect the points; use attributes of shapes to determine what shape is formed

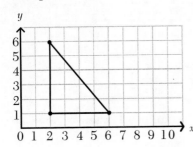

Week 35: Day 3 (page 185)

1. Possible answer: (1, 3) and (6, 2)

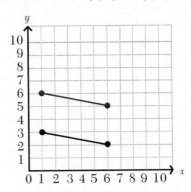

2. Yes, there can be more than one correct solution. Possible explanation: There are many possible parallel lines that would not intersect with the original line.

Week 35: Day 4 (page 186)

1. The playground is located at (4, 2) and the frozen yogurt shop is located at (8, 9). One path is to move right 4 spaces and up 7 spaces. Another path is to move up 7 spaces and to the right 4 spaces.

2. Possible answer: No, one path is not better than the other. Both paths will get you from one location to the other location in the same amount of units.

Week 35: Day 5 (page 187)

1. Level A Wendell:

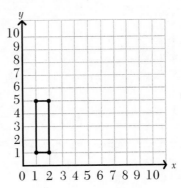

2. Level B Wendell is twice as wide as Level A Wendell, but equally as tall:

Level B	
x	*y*
2	1
4	1
4	5
2	5

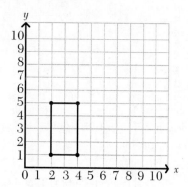

2. Level C Wendell is equally as wide as Level A Wendell, but twice as tall:

Level C	
x	*y*
1	2
2	2
2	10
1	10

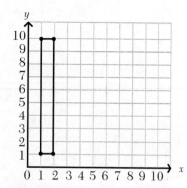

Week 36: Day 1 (page 188)

1. Two more points because a parallelogram has four angles and four sides.

2. Yes, there is more than one way to solve the problem, as long as a parallelogram is formed using the line segment.

3. Parallelograms have 4 sides, 4 angles, opposite sides equal, opposite angles equal, and opposite sides parallel.

Week 36: Day 2 (page 189)

1. Possible answer: (5, 2) and (3, 5); Plot the points given, and add two points to make a parallelogram.

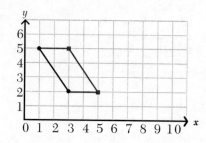

2. Possible answer: (6, 5); Plot the points given, and add one point to make a triangle.

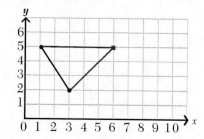

Week 36: Day 3 (page 190)

Jennifer has $16 left after 3 frozen yogurts. She has $7 left after 6 frozen yogurts. She will need to put more money on her card after 8 frozen yogurts.

Frozen yogurts	Dollars
0	25
1	22
2	19
3	16
4	13
5	10
6	7
7	4
8	1

Jennifer's Frozen Yogurt Card

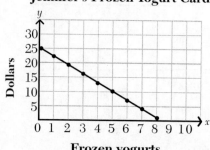

Frozen yogurts

ANSWER KEY *(cont.)*

Week 36: Day 4 (page 191)

1. Possible answers: Rectangle 1: (3, 1) and (3, 4); Rectangle 2: (7, 1) and (7, 4)

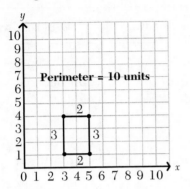

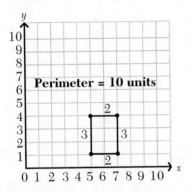

2. Possible answer: I know that the line segment is 3 units long. I need to make another parallel side for the rectangle that is 3 units long. That gives me 6 units so far. I know that the other pair of sides must be equal and parallel. Since there are 4 units left, these sides need to be each 2 units long to make the perimeter 10 units total.

Week 36: Day 5 (page 192)

1. Violet will have enough money after 13 hours. She started with $20 and after 13 hours worked, she has $111 total. She only needs $110 to buy the skateboard, so she has $1 left over.

Hours worked (x)	Dollars saved (y)
0	20
1	27
2	34
3	41
4	48
5	55
6	62
7	69
8	76
9	83
10	90
11	97
12	104
13	111

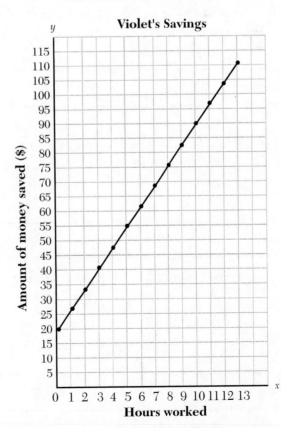

Violet's Savings

PRACTICE PAGE RUBRIC

Directions: Evaluate student work in each category by choosing one number in each row. Students have opportunities to score up to four points in each row and up to 16 points total.

	Advanced	**Proficient**	**Developing**	**Beginning**
Problem-solving strategies	Uses multiple efficient strategies Uses a detailed and appropriate visual model	Uses appropriate strategies Uses an appropriate visual model	Demonstrates some form of strategic approach Uses a visual model but is incomplete	No strategic approach is evident No visual model is attempted
Points	4	3	2	1
Mathematical knowledge	Provides correct solutions and multiple solutions when relevant Connects and applies the concept in complex ways	Provides correct solutions Demonstrates proficiency of concept	Shows some correct solutions Demonstrates some proficiency of concept	No solutions are correct Does not demonstrate proficiency of concept
Points	4	3	2	1
Explanation	Explains and justifies thinking thoroughly and clearly	Explains and justifies thinking	Explains thinking but difficult to follow	Offers no explanation of thinking
Points	4	3	2	1
Organization	Well-planned, well-organized, and complete	Shows a plan and is complete	Shows some planning and is mostly complete	Shows no planning and is mostly incomplete
Points	4	3	2	1

PRACTICE PAGE ITEM ANALYSIS

Directions: Record students' rubric scores (page 214) for the Day 5 practice page in the appropriate columns. Add the totals and record the sums in the Total Scores column. You can view: (1) which students are not understanding the mathematical concepts and problem-solving steps, and (2) how students progress after multiple encounters with the problem-solving process.

Student Name	Week 1	Week 2	Week 3	Week 4	Week 5	Week 6	Week 7	Week 8	Week 9	Total Scores
Average Class Score										

PRACTICE PAGE ITEM ANALYSIS *(cont.)*

Directions: Record students' rubric scores (page 214) for the Day 5 practice page in the appropriate columns. Add the totals and record the sums in the Total Scores column. You can view: (1) which students are not understanding the mathematical concepts and problem-solving steps, and (2) how students progress after multiple encounters with the problem-solving process.

Student Name	Week 10	Week 11	Week 12	Week 13	Week 14	Week 15	Week 16	Week 17	Week 18	Total Scores
Average Class Score										

PRACTICE PAGE ITEM ANALYSIS *(cont.)*

Directions: Record students' rubric scores (page 214) for the Day 5 practice page in the appropriate columns. Add the totals and record the sums in the Total Scores column. You can view: (1) which students are not understanding the mathematical concepts and problem-solving steps, and (2) how students progress after multiple encounters with the problem-solving process.

Student Name	Week 19	Week 20	Week 21	Week 22	Week 23	Week 24	Week 25	Week 26	Week 27	Total Scores
Average Class Score										

PRACTICE PAGE ITEM ANALYSIS *(cont.)*

Directions: Record students' rubric scores (page 214) for the Day 5 practice page in the appropriate columns. Add the totals and record the sums in the Total Scores column. You can view: (1) which students are not understanding the mathematical concepts and problem-solving steps, and (2) how students progress after multiple encounters with the problem-solving process.

Student Name	Week 28	Week 29	Week 30	Week 31	Week 32	Week 33	Week 34	Week 35	Week 36	Total Scores
Average Class Score										

STUDENT ITEM ANALYSIS

Directions: Record individual student's rubric scores (page 214) for each practice page in the appropriate columns. Add the totals and record the sums in the Total Scores column. You can view: (1) which concepts and problem-solving steps the student is not understanding and (2) how the student is progressing after multiple encounters with the problem-solving process.

Student Name:	Day 1	Day 2	Day 3	Day 4	Day 5	Total Scores
Week 1						
Week 2						
Week 3						
Week 4						
Week 5						
Week 6						
Week 7						
Week 8						
Week 9						
Week 10						
Week 11						
Week 12						
Week 13						
Week 14						
Week 15						
Week 16						
Week 17						
Week 18						
Week 19						
Week 20						
Week 21						
Week 22						
Week 23						
Week 24						
Week 25						
Week 26						
Week 27						
Week 28						
Week 29						
Week 30						
Week 31						
Week 32						
Week 33						
Week 34						
Week 35						
Week 36						

PROBLEM-SOLVING FRAMEWORK

Use the following problem-solving steps to help you:

1. understand the problem

2. make a plan

3. solve the problem

4. check your answer and explain your thinking

What Do You Know?

- read/reread the problem

- restate the problem in your own words

- visualize the problem

- find the important information in the problem

- understand what the question is asking

What Is Your Plan?

- draw a picture or model

- decide which strategy to use

- choose an operation (+, −, ×, ÷)

- determine if there is one step or multiple steps

Solve the Problem!

- carry out your plan

- check your steps as you are solving the problem

- decide if your strategy is working or choose a new strategy

- find the solution to the problem

Look Back and Explain!

- check that your solution makes sense and is reasonable

- determine if there are other possible solutions

- use words to explain your solution

PROBLEM-SOLVING STRATEGIES

Draw a picture or diagram.	**Make a table or list.**	**Use a number sentence or formula.**
		$10 + 4 = 14$ $A = l \times w$
Make a model.	**Look for a pattern.**	**Act it out.**
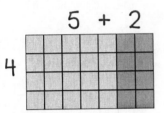	 3, 6, 9, 12, 15, __18__	
Solve a simpler problem.	**Work backward.**	**Use logical reasoning.**
$7 + 6$ $7 + 3 + 3$ $(7 + 3) + 3$ $10 + 3 = 13$	$\boxed{} \times 3 \times 5 = 30$	
Guess and check.	**Create a graph.**	**Use concrete objects.**
$2 \times \boxed{} + 5 = 13$ $2 \times 4 + 5 = 13$ $13 = 13$ Yes!	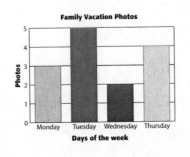	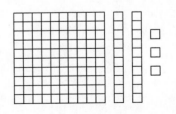 base-ten blocks

DIGITAL RESOURCES

Teacher Resources

Resource	Filename
Practice Page Rubric	rubric.pdf
Practice Page Item Analysis	itemanalysis.pdf itemanalysis.docx itemanalysis.xlsx
Student Item Analysis	studentitem.pdf studentitem.docx studentitem.xlsx

Student Resources

Resource	Filename
Problem-Solving Framework	framework.pdf
Problem-Solving Strategies	strategies.pdf

NOTES

NOTES

#51617—180 Days of Problem Solving